GARDEN OF THE SOULS

Rebbe Nachman

on Suffering

D1546363

Second Edition

For further information, contact:

Breslov Research Institute
POB 5370
Jerusalem, Israel 91053

Breslov Research Institute
POB 587
Monsey, New York 10952

or:
Breslov Research Institute
POB 11
Lakewood, NJ 08701 USA

e-mail: info@breslov.org
INTERNET: http//www.breslov.org

Garden of the Souls

Rebbe Nachman on Suffering

Translated and Edited by Avraham Greenbaum

PUBLISHED BY

THE BRESLOV RESEARCH INSTITUTE

This book is dedicated

in honor of my beloved Papa, HaShem,
who has given me everything I could dream
of and more. Your love and faithfulness are
mind boggling. Thank you for being my Father,
for always being there for me, and for letting
me be your spoiled child. I will always be at
your Shabbos table. I love You.

And to my beloved husband Netzach for the
balance and love he has filled my life with.

And to my children Miriam Ruth and Hillel
Anschel. Thank you for being my children.
I exist for you and would be nothing
without you. Never stray from Hashem
and He will keep you close.

May they all be blessed with joy, happiness,
and abundant blessings, and may they merit
to see the coming of Moshiach. Amen.

Chana Rivka Michel

Table of Contents

FOREWORD

Rebbe Nachman once remarked: "Everyone says there is This World and the World to Come. We believe that the World to Come exists. It could be that This World also exists — somewhere. But here? From the suffering everyone goes through the whole time, it would appear that this is Gehenom." (Likutey Moharan II:119.)

Pain and suffering are with us in so many different ways. Besides our own trials and those of the people around us, our whole generation still lives in the shadow of the Holocaust, an event which poses the most baffling questions on a vast scale and with chilling sharpness. For many people, the fact of suffering is a major obstacle to faith. People say, "How could God let this happen? If this could happen, how could there be a God?"

Rebbe Nachman himself suffered intensely during much of his life. He had to confront the difficult questions face to face. But he was not afraid of them, because, as he said, "I am a 'Know what to answer the non-believer' " (Tzaddik #418.)

What does it mean when an outstanding Torah Sage and Tzaddik tells us this world of suffering is Gehenom? The truth is, it is a message of hope. Gehenom is an awesome concept. Yet Gehenom is a part of God's creation. It is the place where fallen souls are sent, not to be vindictively tormented for no purpose, but to be purified, so that they too will be able to rise up and receive of the goodness of God.

Faith and hope are the keynotes of the teaching that is the centerpiece of this book, Rebbe Nachman's beautiful and evocative lesson, "Garden of the Souls" (Likutey Moharan I:65). Born out of his own grief over the tragic loss of his baby son, Shlomo Ephraim, it offers guidance and comfort in dealing with pain and suffering. The essential point that emerges is that suffering is sent with the purpose of bringing us closer to God. When we firmly believe and know this, we can find ways of using even pain and adversity to draw ourselves closer to the ultimate, joyous goal of life.

Also included is a selection of other teachings of Rebbe Nachman on related themes, and some of the prayers written by the Rebbe's closest pupil, Rabbi Nathan — because what we most need to do when confused, bewildered and confronted with pain and suffering is to turn to God in prayer.

Owing to the great distance of so much of today's world from faith, even the fundamentals of the Torah view of pain and suffering are unfamiliar to many people. An overview has therefore been included at the beginning of the book — "A Matter of Faith" — to introduce some of the central ideas underlying the Torah viewpoint. For those interested in further details, the chapter on "The Torah View of Suffering" contains extracts from "Derech HaShem: The Way of God", by Rabbi Moshe Chaim Luzzatto (the RaMChaL) translated by Rabbi Aryeh Kaplan, and reprinted here with the kind permission of Feldheim Publishers, Jerusalem. The RaMChaL was a brilliant systematizer of Jewish thought, and the passages quoted give the distilled essence of classic Torah teaching on the subject.

Rebbe Nachman's teaching of "Garden of the Souls" is filled with hope and yearning for Mashiach, the Comforter, and for the great good God has in store for us in the end. It is my prayer that we will witness the coming of Mashiach very soon in our times, and quickly see how God will "swallow up death forever and wipe the tears off all faces." (Isaiah 25:8)

Avraham Greenbaum
Jerusalem, Menachem Av 5749

THE BITTER HERB

Rebbe Nachman related:

Once a Jew and a German were travelling as hoboes together. The Jew told the German to pretend he was a Jew (since German and Yiddish are fairly similar), and the Jews would have pity on him. Passover was approaching, so he taught him how to act when invited to a Seder. He told him that at every Seder they make Kiddush over wine, wash the hands, etc. The only thing he forgot to tell him about was the Maror, the bitter herb.

The German was invited to a house, and being very hungry he was looking forward to all the fine foods the Jew had described. The first thing they gave him was a piece of celery dipped in salt water. Next they began to recite the Haggadah, and he sat there longing for the meal. When the matzah was finally served, he was very happy.

Then they gave him a piece of horseradish for the bitter herb. It was extremely bitter, and he thought this was the entire meal. He ran out of the house, bitter and hungry, saying to himself "Cursed Jews! After all that ceremony, that's all they serve to eat!"

He went to the synagogue and fell asleep. Later on the Jew arrived, happy and full from a good meal. "How was your Seder?" he asked. The other one told him what had happened.

"Stupid German!" replied the Jew. "If you had waited just a little longer, you would have had a fine meal, just like me."

The same is true when one wants to come close to God. After all the effort to begin, one is given a little bitterness.

This is necessary in order to purify the body. People might think this bitterness is all there is to serving God, and they run away from it. But if one were to wait a short while and allow the body to be purified, one would feel every joy and delight in the world in one's closeness to God.

Rabbi Nachman's Stories #23

1

A MATTER OF FAITH

When a person understands that everything that happens to them is for their own good, this is a glimpse of the World to Come.

Likutey Moharan I:4

"Fiends, why are you torturing us for nothing?"

In his story of "The Sophisticate and the Simpleton", Rebbe Nachman tells how the Sophisticate proves to his own satisfaction that there is no King over the world. Afire with the zeal of the self-righteous, the Sophisticate sets off with a companion on a world-wide mission to try to persuade everyone else of this "truth". They lose everything they have, but still the Sophisticate refuses to admit he might be wrong.

Finally, the Devil sends for them. The Sophisticate ridicules the idea of the Devil — he no more believes in evil than in good. But to back down from accepting the Devil's dare would mean an unacceptable loss of face. So the Sophisticate has to go off with his companion together with the Devil's messenger.

Rebbe Nachman relates: "The Devil captured the Sophisticate and his companion, and brought them to a quicksand bog. The Devil sat on a throne in the middle of this bog, and he threw the Sophisticate and his companion into the mud. The bog was thick and sticky like glue, and they could not move at all in it.

"When the Devil and his cohorts began to torture these two sophisticates, they screamed out, 'Fiends! Why are you torturing us? Does such a thing as the Devil really exist? You are fiends, and you are torturing us for nothing.' These two sophisticates still did not believe in the Devil. They thought these were wicked people, who were torturing them for no reason..." (Rabbi Nachman's Stories p.193)

The Sophisticate had made it his life's purpose to deny God. He is the exemplar of skepticism, the opposite of faith. In place of the King he has put *himself* on the throne. Spurning external authority and tradition, *he* is going to be the arbiter of what exists. The Sophisticate will believe nothing unless he can see it with his own eyes or understand it with human reason. For him, there is only one world, the one he can look at, touch and feel, the world of nature. He will not admit that levels of spiritual mystery might exist that could be invisible to him.

A world with no King is a world without order — a world of chance, with no such thing as absolute good and evil, no reward for righteousness and punishment for sin. And thus when suffering comes to the Sophisticate, he can find no meaning in it. Having thrown away the idea of Divine Justice, he cannot relate his suffering to what he has done. He cannot learn or grow from it. Being unable to explain it, he finds it pointlessly cruel. And because the Sophisticate has turned his back on God, God turns His back on him, as it were, hiding His unity, punishing him through a devlish plurality of bizarre, meaningless forces: "You are fiends, and you are torturing us for nothing!"

It is his own self that is blinding the Sophisticate to the truth. This is why he has to be punished for so long. Only when he is totally battered down and crushed will he be forced to admit defeat — to admit that there *is* a power greater than himself. At the end of the story, when he sees he is unable to help himself, the Sophisticate finally realizes that only through the intervention of a saintly Miracle Worker could he be saved. "...And he was forced to admit to the truth, that *there is a King*." (ibid. p.195.)

The quicksand bog — what a graphic metaphor for some of the things people go through in this world! How many times in life do we find ourselves stuck: no matter which way we try, twist and turn, we are just caught in thick mud, unable to get free.

And how do we respond? Well we're only human. A Sophisticate nags away in the heart: "Why? Why? ... This is not *fair*! ... What did I do to deserve this? ... Why do You do this to me? If this is what You do, why should I believe in You? Why should I keep to Your rules?"

How much of life goes on anger, complaints, protests, rancour, recriminations, bitterness, hatred. How much energy gets spent on vain struggles against windmills, endless campaigns against the apparent perpertrators of the wrongs and injustices people feel they have suffered. "Fiends, you are torturing us for nothing!"

"Everything God does is for the best"

At the other end of the spectrum is Rabbi Akiva, exemplar of faith. The Talmud relates how once Rabbi Akiva went on a journey. He came to a town and asked if anyone could put him up for the night. The inhospitable inhabitants all refused. Still, Rabbi Akiva said, כל דעביד רחמנא לטב עביד (Kol de-avid Rachmana, le-tov avid) — "Everything God does is for the best," and he went and spent the night in the field. With him he had a lamp, a rooster to wake him and a donkey to ride on. But a wind came and blew out the light, a cat came and ate his rooster, and a lion came and ate the donkey. Rabbi Akiva was left all alone in the dark, but he still said, "Everything God does is for the best."

In the middle of the night a band of marauders came, sacked the town and took all the inhabitants captive. Then Rabbi Akiva said, "Now I see how everything the Holy One does is for the best. If my lamp had been alight, they would have seen me. If the rooster had crowed and the donkey had brayed, they would have known where I was and taken me as well" (Berachot 60b).

A story not about suffering, perhaps — at least, as far as Rabbi Akiva is concerned — but certainly one about things not going as planned. Yet Rabbi Akiva is a believer. Not just intellectually. His belief has a practical effect on the way he conducts his life and responds to what happens to him. He has the humility to accept that a force higher than himself controls the world in general and his life in particular. Belief does not mean that Rabbi Akiva succumbs to passivity and resignation. No, he is a doer — he has lots of plans and he tries doing whatever he can. But when things don't go the way he thought they should, he doesn't get annoyed. He puts up with a bit of inconvenience — because he believes God knows better than he does how to run things.

Rabbi Akiva calls God רחמנא (Rachmana) — the Loving One. No matter what happens, the Loving One is working everything out for the best, even when Rabbi Akiva can least see how. And in the end it was indeed revealed how the hand of Providence had been working at every stage to do what was necessary to save the Tzaddik from the punishment of the wicked.

The Talmud tells us Rabbi Akiva spent the night "in the field". Perhaps the Supernal Field, the Garden of the Souls Rebbe Nachman speaks of in his lesson — the ultimate, joyous goal of all of life. Closing his eyes to the hardships of the physical world, Rabbi Akiva takes himself off to the "field": he focusses his inner eye on the spiritual world of Unity.

Rabbi Akiva was a living expression of Emunah, our faith in the One God as we express it every day in the Shema: Hear, Israel, HaShem, Our God, HaShem is One. God in Himself is beyond any comprehension. He reveals Himself to the world through different facets. There are the aspects of Chesed, Mercy, alluded to in the name HaShem (YKVK), and Gevurah, Might, Strict Judgement, alluded to in the name Elokim. In the Shema we assert that the two facets are one: HaShem is Elokim. Elokim is HaShem. HaShem is One.

Life has different sides. Sometimes things smile at us and we see the Mercy. Other times we feel under a cloud, nothing goes the way we want it, things seem bad. But in the Shema we express our faith that One God is in control of all the different sides of life. Even the hard things in life are from God. When things go differently from the way we might want, it doesn't mean that life is cruel without purpose. Hardship and suffering are not arbitrary. They come from God as much as the good things.

God is Rachmana, the Loving One. Everything He does to us is for our ultimate good. God is perfection, and the greatest love is that we should come close to Him and know Him. But we are like growing children who still want to be little: we don't like leaving behind our childhood indulgences — materialism — for the sake of maturity — the life of the spirit. The worldly ego says "I want things *my* way". But good parents know that if you love your child you have to be firm. You have to deny the child things that will be bad in the long run, and you have to push the child to make an effort to attain the things that will be good.

The hand of Strict Judgement operates in unity with the side of Tender Mercy. Both complement each other, working towards the same goal — the bestowal of God's love on us, which means the revelation of Himself. God is One — אחד — EChaD. The sum of the numerical values of these letters — the gematria — is 13. This is the same as the gematria of אהבה — AHaVaH — Love. Thirteen attributes of Lovingkindness. Perfect unity.

When we say the Shema, the declaration of our faith, we put our hand over our eyes and close them tight. This material world was set up to challenge us. Things cannot be taken at face value here — appearances can be very deceptive.

God is often so hidden, especially when things are bad, and we cannot see where any of it is leading. We close our eyes tight and cover them over with our hand, so as to focus the inner eye on the world of truth. Shema Yisrael, HaShem is Elokim. Elokim is HaShem. Mercy involves Firmness. Firmness is a part of Mercy. HaShem is One.

Why do people suffer?

All this is very fine as long as things are going reasonably well, and the level of suffering is tolerable. A single night without lights, alarm clock, or transportation may be bearable. In Rabbi Akiva's case the meaning of the mysterious happenings of the night was revealed the very next morning. But how many things in this world work out with a happy ending so quickly?

People go through protracted periods of acute suffering, physical and mental. There are so many different kinds of suffering — לא עלינו — *lo alenu* — please, please, not on us! There are all kinds of illnesses, terrible accidents, tragic losses, catastrophic reverses, the shattering of hopes and dreams, whether in families, relationships, careers, businesses. There is the suffering that comes directly from HaShem, and the suffering that is channeled through the agency of others — criminals, persecutors, and even unwitting innocents. We go through suffering ourselves, we see those around us, our loved ones, going through it. And too often we see no happy ending at all in this world — only tragedy, loss, heartache and grief.

Physical pain can sometimes be eased. There may be a cure, or at least the agony can be lessened with pain-killers. But what about the anguish of the soul? So many of the things people go through seem so incomprehensible. It might be easier to accept if we could see something that made clear sense in terms of human logic: suffering as the punishment for evil, the wicked suffer, the good do not. Things are nothing like so simple. Suffering afflicts not only the wicked, but good, upright, hard-working citizens, and even the greatest Tzaddikim. What did the six million victims of the Holocaust do — men, women, children, babies in arms? We are not atheists. We want to believe. But how? How can we begin to understand any of this, let alone accept it?

Silence... and an echo of a voice

At the end of his life, Rabbi Akiva himself suffered the most terrible martyrdom. He was flayed alive at the hands of the Roman oppressors. Rabbi Akiva was undoubtedly a Tzaddik Gamur, a Perfect Tzaddik: a saint, a towering scholar of the Holy Torah, an outstanding leader of his people. *He* has to go through such suffering? Suffering that baffles his students, that baffles Moshe Rabbenu, that baffles the very angels...?

Yet at the climax of his ordeal, Rabbi Akiva is saying "Shema Yisra'el". Wracked with pain, face to face with the most horrible death, Rabbi Akiva asserts the unity of God. Even in his pain and torment he sees the hand of God. How?

There is no answer.

And there is an answer.

And both are correct.

The Talmud (Menachot 29b) depicts Moshe ascending on high and seeing the soul of Rabbi Akiva, who was to plumb greater depths in Moshe's Torah than even Moshe himself. "Show me his reward!" asks Moshe — and he is shown a vision of Rabbi Akiva being flayed alive with iron combs. "Is this the reward for Torah?" asks Moshe. And God replies, "Be silent! This is the way it arose in the Divine thought." Be silent. It is part of the Divine plan. How? Why? No answer. Only silence. Everything is cloaked in mystery.

But the Talmud gives us another dimension of Rabbi Akiva's martyrdom. In Berachot 61b we are told how when Rabbi Akiva was taken out to be killed, it was time for saying

"Shema". Rabbi Akiva was taking on himself the kingship of Heaven. His students ask him "Rabbenu, this too?" And Rabbi Akiva answers: "All my days I've been troubled about this verse — 'love God... with all your soul'— which means 'even if He takes your soul'. I said, When will I have the opportunity to fulfil it? Now that the moment has come, shall I not fulfil it?" Rabbi Akiva drew out the word Echad ... until his soul went out on Echad.

The Talmud continues: The Ministering Angels asked God, "Is this the reward for Torah?" Exactly the same question as Moshe's. Only this time there is an answer. Moshe Rabbenu was flesh and blood — a man living in this world, where life ends with death, and beyond death nothing is visible. But the angels are pure spirit, they are not subject to death, and can therefore understand something which mortal man, this side of death, cannot.

To the angels God gave an answer: "Their portion is *life*..." And a Bat Kol — the "Echo of a Voice" — the distant voice of prophetic intuition — came forth, spelling out the answer for those willing to hear it: "Happy are you, Rabbi Akiva, for you are called to the life of the World to Come!" Such martyrs and sufferers may suffer in *this* world, but ultimately they inherit *life*, the *true* life of the World to Come. Eternal life.

For Moshe, in this world, there was no answer — because in terms of this world alone there can be no answer. If we look at suffering only in the perspective of this visible, temporary world, it must remain incomprehensible. If our only criteria of success and happiness are those of this world — material wealth and pleasures — how can we possibly come to terms with sickness, pain, loss, destruction...? Too often the older people get the more they seem under attack — lonely, bereft of their dear ones, incapacitated, ever more helpless, riddled with aches, pains, chronic disease. Is this where life leads to and nothing more?

The answer is that the purpose lies *beyond* this world, in a realm we cannot see with our physical eyes — a realm only the angels can begin to "see". The most that can be revealed in this world is through a Bat Kol — a faint echo of a voice — the voice of Torah wisdom — for those willing to hear it. It is a matter of belief. It has to be, because this side of death we cannot see what lies beyond. Here we cannot see that for the soul there is no death, only eternal life.

Belief in the World to Come is the foundation of Torah teaching about the meaning of suffering — and indeed of all the different things people go through in this world. (For further details, see next chapter, "The Torah View of Suffering".) This world is the ante-chamber, the place of preparation, leading to the World to Come. Only when we understand that the soul is living and enduring, that its sojourn in a transitory body in a transitory world is a preparation for something higher, can we can begin to make sense of the things people go through in this world.

"He's laughing!"

A funeral procession was passing in front of Rebbe Nachman's window. The people in the procession were crying and wailing. But the Rebbe commented, "Presumably the dead man is laughing in his heart at the way they're crying over him. When someone dies, people cry over him as if to say: How good if you had lived in this world even longer and suffered even more trials and torments, and then you would have had even more bitterness... At least this will be the end of his pain and suffering, because once he has gone through anything he might have to go through [in Gehenom] he will enjoy the reward for his good deeds in this world." (Tzaddik #446.)

So the World to Come is the place of laughter and joy — does that mean we have to wait till then to be happy? Are we supposed to just grit our teeth and bear the pains of this world in the meantime? Could that be the message of Rebbe Nachman of Breslov — who taught the world to rejoice, that "It's a great mitzva to be happy all the time" — ?

Well, what *is* the happiness Rebbe Nachman is teaching us? Much of the world is obsessed with a hell-bent pursuit of the blithe, breezy light-headedness that adverts, films, romances and the like parade as happiness. But even if it exists, it is only a fool's paradise, good as long as reality can be held at bay. This has nothing to do with the holy joy and happiness — the Simchah — that Rebbe Nachman is teaching us. The power and depth of true Simchah is that it is founded on facing reality, not evading it.

We are not supposed to wait for the next world until we can be happy. There is a way to find joy even amidst the suffering of this world — through *belief* in the World to Come. The stronger our belief in it, and the more we work for it and look forward to it, the more we can accept and rejoice in the trials of this world — because we believe, we *know*, that their ultimate purpose is good. We discover the real good that is in this world. This is the essence of Rebbe Nachman's message to us in "Garden of the Souls".

"For the ultimate goal is completely good, and in the end everything will turn out to have been for good. Even when bad things happen and you are beset with troubles and suffering, God forbid, if you will look at the ultimate purpose, you will see these things are not bad at all, they are actually a very great favor. All suffering is sent from God intentionally for your own ultimate good. It could be to remind you to return to God, or to cleanse and scour you of your sins. If so, suffering is really very beneficial. God's intention is certainly only for good.

"Whatever evil and suffering you go through, God forbid, if you will just look at the ultimate goal — God's purpose — you will not experience it as suffering at all. On the contrary, you will be filled with joy at so much good when you look at the purpose of this suffering. Because the ultimate purpose is entirely good, all unity. And the deep truth is, there is no evil at all in the world: everything is good.

"Then why do we feel pain when we suffer? The pain people go through because of their suffering is only because their Da'at — divine understanding — is taken from them, and they are unable to focus on the ultimate purpose, which is entirely good. It is then that they feel the pain and sorrow of their suffering. But when understanding is present and one keeps one's attention on the ultimate goal, one does not feel pain and suffering at all." (Likutey Moharan I:65,3)

What is Da'at? "*VeyoDA'to — Know* today and take it to your heart that HaShem is Elokim — in heaven above and on the earth below — there is none other" (Deuteronomy 4:39). Know: HaShem is Elokim. The two facets of life — Chesed, Mercy, and Gevurah, Might and Strict Judgement — are one. HaShem is Elokim. Elokim is HaShem. HaShem is One. It's a matter of faith. The faith of Rabbi Akiva. When problems came up, he said "Everything the Loving One does is for the best". And at the moment of excruciating pain and torment, he closed his eyes completely to this world in a supreme effort to focus only on the truth beyond it: "Shema Yisrael, HaShem Elokenu HaShem Echad".

The Rabbis (Pesachim 50a) asked about the prophecy "On that day HaShem will be one and His name one" (Zecharia 14:9.) "Why 'on that day'? Isn't God one today?" And they answered that today, for good things we bless God as "good and beneficent", while for bad things we bless Him as "true Judge". In other words, in this world, we do instinctively distinguish between the different facets of life, between good and bad. The underlying unity is for the most part concealed. But in future, said the Rabbis — "on that day" — we will bless God for everything as "good and beneficent"! In the future, in the World to Come, even God's severity will be revealed as an aspect of His love. Everything will be seen to be a single unity.

Da'at means taking the longer perspective — understanding the real place of this world and the things that happen in it in the total scheme of things. Thus when we relate the bad things that happen to our ultimate purpose, when we believe determinedly that they are for our good, we can get a glimpse even here and now of the inexpressible joy of the World to Come. This is the meaning of Rebbe Nachman's saying: "When a person understands that everything that happens to them is for their own good, this is a glimpse of the World to Come — *Me-eyn Olam Haba*." (Likutey Moharan I:4)

Olam Haba itself is beyond this world — "No eye has seen it" (Isaiah 64:3) — because it cannot be seen with the physical eye. We have to close our physical eyes to the outward appearance of this world, and focus our thoughts on the ultimate purpose — Unity. Then we can have *me-eyn Olam Haba* — a fleeting glimpse, an indescribable taste! The word *me-eyn* literally means "from the eye" — signifying the appearance of something. We can have a fleeting glimpse of the way things "look" in the future world. And the hint as to how is: *me-eyn*, "from the eye". Where are our eyes? How do we look at things?

"I never had a bad day in my whole life"

After all the teachings and explanations about the way we are supposed to respond to the hard knocks and blows of life, the practical question still remains: How? How do you look on the good side when the pain *hurts*? "When a person *understands* that everything that happens is for their own good..." Is it possible to understand this at the moment of actual suffering, when the ultimate purpose is far beyond our range of vision?

Let's not even talk about trying to achieve the high level of having clear *knowledge* that things are all for the good. Say we just want to *believe* it even without being able to see it. It's one thing to believe in theory. How do we get the belief into our hearts and respond accordingly? It may be a lot to expect to experience joy at the height of pain, but let's talk about less intense suffering. In more normal circumstances, when things go against us in the way they do one way or another practically every day of our lives, how can we learn to accept the superiority of the Divine wisdom with love? How can we remain cheerful and happy instead of kicking, screaming and complaining? How, in this benighted world, can we learn to look at the things we don't like differently?

A man once came with these very same questions to Rabbi Dov Ber, the Magid of Mezritch: "How can I learn to accept the bad things in life?" And the Magid said to him: "I have a disciple who will be able to help you. His name is Reb Zusya. He lives in such and such a place. Go to him."

The man found a low, broken-down house betraying all the signs of extreme poverty and suffering. When Reb Zusya appeared, the man explained why he had come. "But I don't understand," said Reb Zusya. "Why did the Magid send you to me? I never had a bad day in my whole life!"

A famous Chassidic tale... but did the Reb Zusya of the story really exist? Was the actual Reb Zusya of Anipoli really like that? Could someone in real life live in abject poverty with all that it entails — hunger, deprivation, discomfort, sickness, pain — and be in Gan Eden? Didn't Reb Zusya *feel* the discomfort — when so many people in their luxury villas and mansions, with more food, clothes and money than they themselves could ever need, are mournful, depressed and full of complaints?

Perhaps some of us look at Reb Zusya and say in our hearts, he probably wasn't used to anything better. *I* could never accept anything like that in my life. Is there an element of pride in such a reaction? How demeaning to have to go through that. And fear? Please, God, don't ever do that to me! Maybe we have a sneaking suspicion that learning to look at things differently doesn't really make the pain go away! And in a childish way, isn't that what we really want — that pain and suffering should just disappear? Is Reb Zusya's way of looking at things really a solution?

We may certainly admire Reb Zusya and wonder at his greatness. But what does his example do for *us*? Is such a level practically possible for you and me? How can ordinary people with all their human frailties, needs, desires, standards, etc. possibly experience pain, hardship and adversity as being good?

Perhaps the man who came to the Magid with his questions felt exactly the same way, as he stood there contemplating Reb Zusya. Why did the Magid send me here? What kind of an answer is this supposed to be? Yet the question remains. How *do* we cope with suffering? Because it is with us whether we like it or not.

Self-Centered or God-Centered

You might have thought the Magid should have responded by sending the man home with some kind of practical self-improvement program to deepen his faith. How *was* he supposed to benefit from going to see Reb Zusya?

Well, first let's consider what Reb Zusya really was. He was a living example of *bittul* — one of the key concepts in "Garden of the Souls". The root idea of bittul is to make something into nothing, to nullify or cancel. In the terminology of Mussar and Chassidut, bittul refers to a state of self-surrender and transcendence. One recognizes oneself as a creation of God, dependent on God, a servant of God. Bittul is the opposite of *yeshut*, most ordinary people's regular state, in which they experience themselves as separate and independent entitites, with an outlook and responses that are basically ego-centered.

Pure bittul is not a state that can be experienced permanently in this life. Even to talk about bittul as an experience is somewhat of a contradiction in terms, because "experience" implies that there is someone having the experience, whereas in bittul one is taken quite out of oneself. Rebbe Nachman makes it clear in "Garden of the Souls" (and see Likutey Moharan I:4,9) that even the most advanced spiritual seekers go into bittul only for fleeting moments — at the height of intense prayer and meditation, for example.

Yet there is a more everyday aspect of bittul that everyone is capable of achieving. Step by step, one works towards a fundamental shift of orientation in which self-centeredness is sacrificed for God-centeredness. One learns to accept that God's goals for our lives, as taught in the Torah, are more vitally important than the mundane goals and projects dear to our material egos. God's guidelines about how to make a success of life are truer and more firmly founded than any of the ideas we or those around us could ever think up by ourselves.

Why do we not experience God's goodness at all times if not because our whole attention is focussed on what *we* want and desire, our *own* goals, projects and purposes. We want to control things and have them go *our* way. We get tense, anxious, and fearful that things won't go the way we want. And when they finally don't, we are frustrated, angry, outraged, depressed...

Where are our eyes? Rebbe Nachman teaches: The sun shines constantly, it's just that you can't always see the light because the earth is in the way — even though the earth is very small in comparison with the sun. The "sun" is Godly light — the light of the Torah and the Tzaddikim. The "earth" is earthly materialism — This World, with all its desires and obsessions.

Says Rebbe Nachman: You may be standing facing a great mountain, but if you take even a little coin and hold it in front of your eyes, you won't be able to see the mountain. So it is when we come into this world: we get sunk amidst the vanities of this world and think there's nothing better — because this tiny little world prevents us from seeing the great light of the Torah, which is so many thousands of times greater. The world is there in front of our eyes and stops us from seeing any further. If only we could remove the barriers from in front of our eyes. If only we could lift our heads up a bit and look a little further. We would see such a wonderful light — the light of the Torah and the Tzaddikim — and we would not feel we were missing anything.

"Oy va-voy!" cried the Baal Shem Tov, "The world is full of such incredible radiance, such wonderful secrets... And there's a little hand stuck in front of the eyes, stopping them seeing these great lights." (Likutey Moharan I:133.)

If we could just lift up our heads a bit and look a little further. Bittul in the practical sense means just this — lifting ourselves up so as to see beyond our ego-bound interests and ideas. Little by little one learns to erase the part which says "I want things *this* way. I can only accept things as good if they come out *my* way." And thus one comes to accept that "You decreed it *that* way, and You really do know better."

Reb Zusya had achieved this bittul to perfection. That is how he could accept that everything is from God and therefore good. "I never had a bad day in my whole life."

A Chip at the Ego

Emunah — faith — is the answer, and emunah means taking a different perspective. This may help explain why the Magid didn't just send his questioner home to work on his faith by himself. He had to come *out* of his ego-bound self. That's why he had to go to see a Tzaddik — someone who could *take* him out, and show him a whole other perspective on life. The first step towards Emunah is one of self-deflation. We have to acknowledge that we ourselves do *not* have all the right answers. We do not know. We are not perfect. There are others who are far wiser and saintlier.

The Tzaddik is a kind of spiritual mirror you go to in order to see yourself by comparison and understand where you're really holding (Likutey Moharan I:19,2). This is why Rebbe Nachman's lesson to us in "Garden of the Souls" begins with the idea of leadership. The souls in the Garden cannot grow without the Master of the Field. Only with outside guidance can we rise above ourselves and come to a higher perspective.

The road to bittul can be long and arduous. Really trying to put the Tzaddik's teachings into practice may involve extensive re-evaluation of one's goals and priorities, many doubts and questions, difficult adjustments to habitual patterns and lifestyle, trying new ways, facing challenges, falling down, trying to pick oneself up and start again.

Do the perspectives of Rabbi Akiva or Reb Zusya seem impossibly hard to achieve? That should not deter us from making a start. It was Reb Zusya himself who taught us to be ourselves and start from where we are. "At the Heavenly judgement, I won't be afraid if they ask me why I wasn't like Abraham, Isaac and Jacob. When they ask me, Why weren't you like Reb Zusya — that's when I'll be afraid!"

And who am I? Am I so wise that I know what is really best for me — best in this world and best in terms of my ultimate destiny? Is the way I think things ought to be necessarily the way they should be? Am I entitled to expect that everything should always go exactly the way I want? Have I done right all my life — am I so pure and saintly that nothing needs fixing in my life. Do I understand what needs fixing and how? And when I know things need fixing, do I do everything necessary of my own accord, without needing any kind of push or nudge from the outside?

And for all that, "...Your kindnesses are never exhausted... and Your tender mercies are never ended!"

Who understands the meaning of the suffering in this world — *lo alenu* — please, please, not on us! Who knows who suffers and how? Who understands the pain in another person's heart? Who understands the pain in our own hearts? But there is one kind of suffering we can perhaps do something about: the suffering caused by the Sophisticate in us.

The Sophisticate had dethroned the King and made himself king. That was why he was made to suffer — until his pride was broken down and he finally had to admit: I am not the king. God is the King.

2

THE TORAH VIEW OF SUFFERING

A clear and concise expression of the Torah view of suffering is contained in "Derech HaShem: The Way of God", by R. Moshe Chaim Luzzatto, translated by R. Aryeh Kaplan (Feldheim Publishers, Jerusalem, 1983).

Rabbi Moshe Chaim Luzzatto (1707-46) is usually known as the RaMChaL, from the acronym of his name. An outstanding Torah Sage and Tzaddik, he lived in Italy, Holland and finally Eretz Yisrael, a couple generations before Rebbe Nachman. The RaMChaL's brilliance as a systematizer of traditional Torah teachings is evidenced both in the "Derech HaShem" — a comprehensive outline of Jewish belief — and in the classic Mussar work for which he is most famous, the "Mesilath Yesharim: Path of the Just" (which Rebbe Nachman recommended to some of his followers — see Sichos ve-Sippurim p.167).

Extracts from the "Derech HaShem" are reprinted here by kind permission of Feldheim Publishers.

The purpose of the Creation

To understand the meaning and purpose of suffering, we must first go back to the very purpose of the Creation and the meaning of our life in this world. The Ramchal explains:

God's purpose in creation was to bestow of His good to another. Since God desired to bestow good, a partial good would not be sufficient. The good that He bestows would have to be the ultimate good that His handiwork could accept.

True good exists only in God. His wisdom therefore decreed that the nature of this true benefaction be His giving created things the opportunity to attach themselves to Him to the greatest degree possible for them.

God's wisdom, however, decreed that for such good to be perfect, the one enjoying it must be its master. He must be one who has earned it for himself, and not one associated with it accidentally and without reason.

God therefore arranged and decreed the creation of concepts of both perfection and deficiency, as well as a creature with equal access to both — namely, Man. This creature would then be given the means to earn perfection and avoid deficiency. (pp.37-39.)

Man must earn this perfection, however, through his own free will and desire. If he were compelled to choose perfection, then he would not actually be its master, and God's purpose would not be fulfilled. It was therefore necessary that man be created with free will.

Man's inclinations are therefore balanced between good and evil, and he is not compelled toward either of them. He has the power of choice, and is able to choose either side, knowingly and willingly, as well as to possess whichever one he wishes. Man was therefore created with both a Good Urge (*Yetzer Tov*) and an Evil Urge (*Yetzer Ra*). He has the power to incline himself in whichever direction he desires. (p.45.)

This World and the Next

The true purpose of man's creation was that he should be worthy of attaining true good, namely experiencing God in the World to Come. Man's ultimate destiny is therefore the tranquillity of the Future World. The Highest Wisdom decreed, however, that this would best be attained if man would first exist in the present world, bound and limited by its natural laws. This is actually the true and proper preparation necessary for the desired goal, and everything in this world was therefore arranged so that it should serve as a means of preparing and readying man for this ultimate purpose. (p.95.)

The creation of man with a Good Urge, an Evil Urge and free will allows the human race to include some individuals who are good as well as others who are evil. Ultimately, the evil ones must be cast aside, and the good ones gathered to form one Perfected Community. It is for this Community that the Future World and all its attained goods are intended. (p.95.)

Man's true reward is in the World to Come, and for the worthy individual this consists of the eternal continuous experiencing of God. The ultimate punishment, on the other hand, is that the individual should be deprived of this true good and destroyed.

The judgement was set up, however, to be in accordance with the majority of one's deeds. The good deeds of the wicked and evil deeds of the righteous, which constitute a minority, are dealt with in this world through its gratifications and sufferings. It is in this world that the wicked are rewarded with prosperity for their few virtues, while the righteous are punished with suffering for their few faults.

As a result of this, everyone's judgement is perfect. The Future World likewise remains suitable for its intended perfect state. It is inhabited only by the righteous, and the wicked are totally absent. Those who inhabit the Future World are furthermore free of any obstacle within themselves that might restrict the delight intended for them. The wicked, on the other hand, are cast aside and annihilated, but they have no cause to complain since they have already been rewarded for their few virtues in the present world. (pp.97-99.)

Purification

In His mercy, God maximized man's chances of successfully attaining his ultimate goal. He therefore decreed that there should be another type of purification for those who could benefit from it. It was intended for those who have been surmounted by evil, but not to such a great extent that they should be utterly annihilated.

This purification includes a number of spiritual punishments the most prominent being that of Gehenom (Purgatory). The purpose of these punishments is to penalize the individual for his sins in such a way that he is subsequently free of any liability for the evil that he may have done. As a result, he can then receive the true reward for his good deeds.

Because of this, the number of people who are actually annihilated is small and insignificant. It only consists of those who are dominated by evil so completely that it is utterly impossible for them to have any chance of experiencing the true reward and everlasting delight of experiencing God. (p.99.)

The details of man's judgement, however, are not known to anyone other than God, who is the True Judge. He is the only One who knows the true nature and results of all deeds on every level and in each detail. He therefore knows which should be recompensed in each particular period and manner. (p.99.)

The Purpose of Suffering

Good deeds incorporate an intrinsic quality of perfection and excellence into man's body and soul. Evil deeds, on the other hand, incorporate in him a quality of insensitivity and deficiency, all with a precise measure depending on the deeds, no more and no less.

The righteous man may attain in himself a large measure of brilliance and excellence. From another side, however, because of the minority of evil deeds that he has done, there is in him an admixture of darkness and insensitivity. As long as he still has this admixture, he is neither prepared nor suited to experience God.

The Highest Mercy therefore decreed that some sort of purification exist. This is the general category of suffering.

God gave suffering the power to dispel the insensitivity in man, allowing him to become pure and clear, prepared for the ultimate good at its appointed time. The amount of suffering needed to purify the individual would then depend on the amount of insensitivity that he has acquired as a result of his deeds.

In many cases, it is possible that physical suffering alone would not have the power to dispel this insensitivity, and in such cases, spiritual purification in the Soul World is also necessary. (p.101.)

Suffering may come to an individual in order to make him examine his deeds and motivate him to repent. This is particularly true in the case of a righteous person who may have commited a few sins, or in the case of an intermediate individual, whose sins are balanced by good deeds.

Such suffering, however, is not the same as that discussed earlier, which was an atonement for sin. What we are speaking of now are sufferings meant to motivate a person and awaken his heart to repent.

Punishment was only created to exist in the absence of repentance. What God truly desires is that man not sin in the first place, and if he does sin, that he should repent. If one does not repent, however, he can still be purified through these punishments and thus not be annihilated completely.

Suffering therefore initially comes to an individual to motivate him to repent. If this is not effective, then he must also undergo further suffering to cleanse him of his sins. Regarding this, Elihu told Job (Job 36:10), "[God] opens their ear to discipline, and bids them repent from sin." (pp.115-117.)

Role of the Tzaddikim

When the Highest Wisdom considered everything needed to rectify the human race and make it into the Perfected Community discussed earlier, it saw that this goal would be furthered if some people could benefit others and help them attain a place in this Community.

The rule that the Community of the Future World be restricted only to those who attained perfection in their own right is therefore not absolute. For it was also decreed that an individual can reach a level where he can partake of perfection and be included in this Community as a result of his association with a more worthy individual. The only difference is that he will remain on a lower level, since he is not included in this Community in his own right, but only through association with another.

Those who cause others to partake in the World to Come will definitely be the foremost in that Community. They will be the leaders, while those who enter by vitrtue of their association with them will be beholden to and dependent on them.

In order for this to be possible, all men were originally bound to each other, as our sages teach us, "All Israel are responsible for one another." As a result of this, each individual is bound to everyone else, and no man is counted separately. God's attribute of good is the stronger, however, and if the guilt for sin is shared by others, this must certainly be true of the merit associated with good deeds.

Suffering of the Tzaddikim

As a result of this principle, suffering and pain may be imposed on a Tzaddik (righteous person) as an atonement for his entire generation. This Tzaddik must then accept this suffering with love for the benefit of his generation, just as he accepts the suffering imposed upon him for his own sake. In doing so, he benefits his generation by atoning for it, and at the same time is himself elevated to a very great degree. For a Tzaddik such as this is made into one of the leaders in the Community of the Future World, as discussed earlier.

All this involves a Tzaddik who is stricken because his generation is about to be annihilated, and would be destroyed if not for his suffering. In atoning for them through his suffering, this Tzaddik saves them in this world and greatly benefits them in the World to Come.

The Outstanding Tzaddikim

Within this same category, however, there is a class that is even higher than this. There is suffering that comes to a Tzaddik who is even greater and more highly perfected than the ones discussed above. This suffering comes to provide the help necessary to bring about the chain of events leading to mankind's ultimate perfection.

According to the original plan, the sequence of worldly events required that man undergo at least some suffering before both he and the world could attain perfection. This was required by the very fact that one of the basic concepts of man's predicament was that God should hold back His Light and hide His presence, as discussed earlier. This became all the more necessary as a result of the corruption and spiritual damage caused by man's many sins, which held the good back even more and caused God's presence to become all the more hidden. The world and everything in it are therefore in a degraded evil state, and require that God's unfathmomable wisdom bring about numerous chains of events to achieve their rectification.

Among the most important elements of this sequence is the requirement that man be punished for his wickedness until the attribute of justice is satisified. God arranged matters, however, so that select perfect individuals could rectify things for others, as discussed earlier. The attribute of justice therefore relates to them rather than to the rest of the world in general.

Individuals such as these, however, are themselves perfect, and are therefore worthy only of good. The only reason they suffer is because of others, and the attribute of justice must therefore be as satisfied with a small amount of suffering on their part as with a large amount on the part or those who actually sinned.

Beyond that, the merit and power of these Tzaddikim is also increased because of such suffering, and this gives them even greater ability to rectify the damage of others. They can therefore not only rectify their own generation, but can also correct all the spiritual damage done from the beginning, from the time of the very first sinners.

It is obvious that individuals such as these will ultimately be the foremost leaders in the Perfected Community, and the ones who are the very closest to God. (pp.119-125.)

All this is not only the result of justice, but also follows from the actual order of things, as discussed earlier. As a result of man's sins, corruption is increased and incorporated into both man and the world. This in turn causes God's light to be increasingly retracted and hidden. The more this corruption is cleansed, on the other hand, and the more people are purified of it, the more God's light is once again revealed, step by step.

Suffering is the thing that God created to cleanse this pollution, both in general and in particular. Thus through the suffering of these select individuals, creation in general is cleansed, and step by step the world is brought closer to perfection. (p.125.)

3

A TEACHING BORN OF TEARS

One has to shed tears before one can develop new Torah ideas
of real worth.

Likutey Moharan I:262

Rebbe Nachman never wrote a single text giving a
systematic exposition of all his ideas: that was not his style
of teaching. Whatever he was doing, words of Torah flowed
forth — whether he was sitting with his followers on Shabbos
or festivals, or at casual moments in his house or outside,
walking, travelling, visiting... The Rebbe's very movements
and gestures were Torah. His *life* was Torah — because for
him, Torah and life were the same thing.

The Rebbe's closest follower was Rabbi Nathan (1780-
1844). From the time he first came to the Rebbe in 1802,
Rabbi Nathan had no doubt he was witness to something of
enduring significance not just for himself but for the whole
Jewish People. Rabbi Nathan set himself to record whatever
he could, even Rebbe Nachman's most casual remarks.

Rabbi Nathan wrote detailed accounts of literally
hundreds of different teachings and conversations. Whenever
he could, he would take what he had written to the Rebbe and
check it with him word by word. On occasion Rebbe Nachman
would give Rabbi Nathan his own manuscript version of a
lesson or outline notes. Rabbi Nathan edited and printed
several collections of the Rebbe's teachings, his stories and
conversations, and other anecdotes.

The most important is *Likutey Moharan* — literally
"Collected [Teachings] of Morenu (our teacher) HaRav Rabbi

Nachman", containing some four hundred teachings, including the major lessons Rebbe Nachman gave to his assembled followers especially on the festivals. Then he might speak for three or four hours, elaborating on Torah ideas in a highly structured, subtle and intricate way, with references ranging over the entire Biblical and Rabbinic literature, as well as allusions to various things which were happening both among his followers and in the world at large.

The subject of pain and suffering is touched on by the Rebbe in many different teachings, of which "Garden of the Souls" is one of the most striking and moving. It is printed in Likutey Moharan I:65. The Hebrew version is entitled "And Bo'az said to Ruth", from the verse in Ruth 2:8 which is explained towards the end of the lesson. We have given it the title of "Garden of the Souls" because of the opening theme.

It is a teaching which was born out the Rebbe's own intense pain and suffering. He had known hardship and suffering at many junctures in his life. He had gone through times of extreme poverty. In his journeys to and from Israel he was nearly shipwrecked several times, and at one point was held captive by pirates and almost sold into slavery. After his return to Russia, as his fame began to spread, he became the object of intense opposition and was mercilessly persecuted.

The Rebbe had already lost a young daughter, Feige, in 1804, and another baby daughter had died in infancy. Then, in the Summer of 1806, tragedy struck again. The Rebbe's baby boy, Shlomo Ephraim, who had been born only a year earlier, and for whom he had had the highest hopes, died. Rebbe Nachman took this as a blow not only to himself but to the whole Jewish People, to whom he had devoted his entire life.

The beginning of the 1800's was a time of the greatest significance for all of subsequent Jewish history, as indeed for the future of the world in general. Europe was caught in the grip of the Napoleonic Wars, which brought waves of trauma and change, political and social. At the same time, traditional Jewish life was under attack from within and without. In Austria, Germany, France, Poland and Russia, moves were afoot to try to integrate the Jews not just politically but also culturally in a way which was eventually to undermine the very foundations of Jewish community life and Torah education, leading to assimilation on a scale hitherto unknown.

One of the greatest concentrations of Jews in the world was in Russia itself — her expansion into Poland's eastern provinces since the 1770's had brought over a million Jews under her sovereignty. The first years of the 1800's saw the final shaping of the policy which has effectively governed Russia's dealings with her Jewish population since. They were to be uprooted from their traditional way of life and even from the rural towns and villages they had lived in for centuries. Their separate identity and culture were to be ruthlessly destroyed. They were to be given the same education as non-Jews, to wear the same dress and speak the same language. If they would not do so willingly, they were to be forced.

Rebbe Nachman saw the assault on Jewish education and culture as the most serious threat of all. It would cause future generations to become cut off from even the most basic contact with their heritage. The Jews were under the shadow of a Heavenly decree of the utmost seriousness. Where was the leader who could *do something* about the situation — a leader of outstanding strength and vision, one with the power to inspire and vitalize, to open people's eyes and raise them out of their apathy, a leader who would be able to rectify the damage to the spirit of the Jewish People, the damage to their souls? Where was Mashiach?

Shlomo Ephraim — born in the spring of 1805 — was Rebbe Nachman's first son. Was he to be the leader who would rectify the damage? Was he to be the one to inaugurate the era of Mashiach?

How exactly Rebbe Nachman saw the child's future role is impossible for us to know. Only a Tzaddik could understand what goes into the making of a soul and why it comes down into this world. We know that Rebbe Nachman wanted a son who would take his place after him, but what kind of a dynasty he had in mind will always remain an impenetrable mystery, as will so many other aspects of the life and personality of this towering sage. Speculation would at best be fruitless, and could be very misleading.

Yet one thing that does emerge very clearly from our sources is that Rebbe Nachman closely associated the fate of Shlomo Ephraim with the future of the Jewish People. By the spring of 1806 the child was sick with tuberculosis. The Rebbe asked his followers to pray for him, and he himself prayed, but to no avail. Shortly after Shavuos of 1806 the child died.

Rabbi Nathan writes:
"The Rebbe said the Mashiach had been ready to come a number of years hence and the Rebbe knew exactly which year, which month and on what day he would come. However now he will certainly not come then. From what he said we understood that the reason for the delay was because of the death of his child, Shlomo Ephraim."

Yemey Moharnat 11b

"Shortly after the child's death we were with the Rebbe upstairs in his house. He spoke about the terrrible pain and suffering he had on all sides, within himself and from the world outside. He was seriously ill and suffering intense physical pain. At the same time he had to face unremitting persecution, all of it for no reason — because his opponents had fabricated everything they were accusing him of, and had made up things which had never even entered his mind. All this was in addition to all kinds of other things he was suffering, because the Rebbe was one who suffered constantly.

"As he was speaking, he said to us, 'How can you understand what a tragedy the death of the child is for the world? My whole heart is broken and torn from its place.' Tears began rolling down his cheeks. We felt so ashamed seeing him crying in front of us, we immediately left him and fled. We felt as if the whole world had been destroyed.

"The following day was Friday. The Rebbe said, if we had not gone downstairs the day before, he would have told us something very beautiful. And that Friday he gave a most wonderful Torah teaching — the teaching in Likutey Moharan I:65 — ['Garden of the Souls']."

Yemey Moharnat 11a

It was at this critical juncture in his own life and in the history of the Jewish People that Rebbe Nachman gave the teaching of "Garden of the Souls". After nearly two thousand years of exile, persecution and suffering, all that seemed to be in prospect was more torment, God forbid. What was going to be? When would redemption come?

And what does redemption really mean? Freedom? What kind of freedom? Material milk and honey? That doesn't necessarily bring the world to God. Exile is more than just physical. Our exile is from the garden of the spirit — and true redemption is the redemption of the soul, when the soul is free to rise in ecstatic devotion and attachment to God through Torah and prayer.

When will the redemption come? Where is Mashiach? Who will come to redeem the souls?

4

GARDEN OF THE SOULS

"And Bo'az said to Ruth, 'Please listen, my daughter, don't
go to glean in someone else's field, and also don't pass on from
here... Keep your eyes on the field where they are reaping, and
go behind them. I've told the young men not to touch you.
If you are thirsty, go to the vessels and drink from what the
young men have drawn.' "

(Ruth 2:8-9)

In the Hebrew edition of Likutey Moharan this lesson is
entitled "And Bo'az said to Ruth" — from the verses in the Book
of Ruth which Rebbe Nachman explains towards the end. The
major part of the lesson is devoted to the Rebbe's explanation
and development of his main themes and teachings. These are
presented in a series of *hakdamot* — "introductions" (sections
1-4), each of which leads on to the next. In the light of these
explanations, the Rebbe finally turns to the verses from Ruth
(section 5), showing how all the leading ideas in the lesson are
alluded to in the Hebrew text of the verses.

Study Suggestion: It is probably best to have a broad
sense of the main outline of the lesson before going into the
individual sections in detail. A good way to approach this
lesson might be to first read through the text as a whole a
couple of times without reference to the notes, and without
necessarily expecting to understand every point. For deeper
study later on, the footnotes offer guidelines for interpreting
some of the main ideas, while the next chapter, "Insights"
contains further explanation of the principle themes of the
lesson drawn from the writings of Rabbi Nathan.

Garden of the Souls
Likutey Moharan I:65

There is a field...

The underlying theme of the lesson is the Tachlis — *the ultimate goal of our lives and of the creation in general. This is that all the souls should be perfected in order to enjoy the complete revelation of God's unity. This is expressed in the concept of the Garden of Eden, the idea with which the lesson begins.*

1. KNOW that there is a field where the most beautiful and pleasant trees and herbs grow. The precious beauty of this field and its plants and trees is impossible to describe. Happy is the eye that has seen it![1]

The trees and herbs are the holy souls which grow there. But there are many naked souls[2] roaming and wandering in

---

1. Impossible to describe. Happy is the eye... It is impossible to describe it in the terms of our world of plurality and division because it is a realm where all is unity. Therefore "no eye has seen it" (Isaiah 64:3) — because human vision implies a division between the spectator and the object of vision, whereas to apprehend this realm the subject must surrender self and become merged in God's unity, as explained later in the lesson. Even when one has a vision of Godliness, it cannot be communicated — see Rabbi Nachman's Wisdom #1.

2. Many naked souls. "In the Future World many people will be left outside. They will cry in a bitter voice, 'Give us something to eat! ... What we need is the food of Torah and devotion.' Other people will be left outside naked.

exile outside the field. They are waiting and longing to be fixed, so as to be able to go back in to their places. Sometimes even a great soul, on which many other souls depend, may go outside the field, and it is very hard for it to return. All these souls are waiting expectantly for the Master of the Field who can do what is necessary to restore them. Sometimes a soul is restored through the death of someone[3], or through a mitzva or act of devotion performed by someone.

Anyone who wants to gird his loins and put himself forward as the Master of the Field has to be strong and powerful, a mighty warrior, a man of outstanding wisdom and saintliness. He needs to be on the highest of spiritual levels. There is one Tzaddik who can only complete the task with his own death, and even for this he needs to be very great indeed, because there are many great Tzaddikim who even with their death would not be able to help. Only a Tzaddik on the most outstanding of levels can complete what is necessary in his lifetime. For he has to go through tremendous suffering and hardship[4]. Yet through his greatness he is able to overcome everything and accomplish all that is needed in the field.

When the Master of the Field succeeds in restoring the souls and bringing them in, then it is very good and beautiful

---

They too will cry, 'Give us something to cover ourselves with ... We need Mitzvot and good deeds to cover ourselves with.' " Rabbi Nachman's Wisdom #23.

3. Sometimes a soul is restored through the death of someone. A famous example is that of the *Eser Harugei Malchut*, the ten outstanding Rabbis who suffered cruel martyrdom at the hands of the Romans in order to bring atonement for the Jewish People (see Etz Chaim, Sha'ar Hakavanot, Sefirat HaOmer). See also "Tzaddik: A Portrait of Rabbi Nachman" (BRI) #87 for an account of how the Baal Shem Tov once encountered souls that could only be restored through his death.

4. tremendous suffering and hardship. See the section on The Outstanding Tzaddikim in "The Torah View of Suffering".

to pray. For then prayer attains its perfection[5]. The Master of the Field labors constantly, supervising everything, watering the trees and plants, tending and cultivating them and doing all the other work needed in the field. He sees to it that all the trees are the right distance from one another so that none should overshadow and weaken another. Sometimes it is necessary to put a very close follower at a great distance so that he should not overshadow his friend.

Soul-talk

2. And know that when the souls produce fruit — when they do the will of the Omnipresent — the eyes of the Master of the Field shine[6]. They can then gaze and see to the place where he must look. Then the field is the "field of visionaries" (Numbers 23:14). But when the souls fail to do His will, Heaven forbid, the eyes of the Master of the Field become darkened[7], and then the field is "a field of weepers" (Ohelot

---

5. Prayer attains its perfection. This is the first explicit reference to prayer, which is one of the major themes of the lesson, and is developed in great detail in Section 2 below. Prayer is the basis of all attachment and devotion to God, the gate through which one enters to HaShem and comes to know Him (Likutey Moharan II:84.) Since the purpose of the restoration of the souls is that they should know God, when they are all brought back into the field, prayer is perfected. The elevation of prayer is therefore the main task of the Mashiach — and David, the Messianic king, said of himself "I am prayer" (Psalms 109:4).

6. The eyes of the Master of the Field shine. Again the theme of vision comes in, because everything depends on where we direct our eyes — see below, Section 3.

7. When the souls fail to do His will... the eyes of the Master of the Field become darkened. When people fail to do the will of God or go against it, what is the point of their life? Thus the wicked are not really alive — even in their lifetime they are called "dead" (Berachot 18b) and the field is "a field of weepers". When the souls are far from God, the Tzaddik also falls from his level of perception (cf. Likutey Moharan I:49,7) and "the eyes of the Master of the Field become darkened".

18; Mo'ed Katan 5b referring to a field where funerals stop on the way to the cemetery). For weeping damages one's vision, as the Rabbis taught: " 'And the clouds return after the rain' (Ecclesiastes 12:2) — this refers to vision, which fades as a result of weeping."

But when the field is the "field of visionaries" and the eyes of the Master of the Field are shining, he is able to look into each soul[8] and bring it to its ultimate fulfilment. To know how near or far each soul is from its goal, the indicator is speech — how the person talks. The Master of the Field examines each one's speech[9] to see if it is developed to perfection or not, because this shows if the soul in question is still far from the ultimate goal. The Master of the Field then brings the soul to its goal, until the soul is able to talk perfectly, the way it should.

8. He is able to look into each soul. Cf. Y'arot D'vash I:12: "The Rabbis said, 'The glance of a Tzaddik brings blessing'. The rays of light coming from the eyes of a Tzaddik are a blessing."

9. Speech. The way a person speaks is indicative of his or her spiritual state. The letters and syllables which make up speech are formed by our vocal organs, but the power of the mouth to produce meaningful messages derives from the inner person controlling the physical vocal organs, i.e. the soul. This is the meaning of the statement later on that "when speech comes forth, it comes from the soul."

A person's thoughts are hidden from others (and sometimes even themselves!) Speech reveals that which would otherwise remain hidden. Words are "vessels", the content of the vessels being the meaning that is communicated. The more spiritually developed a person is, the more their words are luminous with Godly awareness and revelation. (Thus Joseph constantly had God's Name on his lips, bringing Godly awareness even to Potiphar. See Rashi on Genesis 39:3.) People who are far from God, on the other hand, talk in a way that conceals Godliness. Lashon Hara, bad language, means not only maligning others and casting aspersions on their Divine souls; it can include talking about events, natural phenomena etc. in a way that hides the Godly wonder that is present in everything in the world. The state of a person's soul is thus reflected in their speech.

Every single word is a whole world. When a person stands up to pray and recites the words of the prayers, he is gathering beautiful flowers and blossoms, like someone going through a meadow picking lovely flowers and blossoms, one by one, until they make a bunch. Then he picks more, one by one, until they make another bunch, and he puts them together. So he goes on, picking and gathering more and more lovely bouquets.

So it is in prayer: one goes from letter to letter, until several letters are joined together to make a syllable. One does the same to make whole words. Then one joins together two words, and goes on, picking and gathering, until one completes a whole blessing. Then one goes on picking more and more, and continues from Avot, the Fathers — the first blessing of the Amida Prayer — to Gevurot, the Godly Powers — the second blessing. Then one goes from Gevurot to Kedushot, Holiness — the third blessing. So one goes on, further and further. Who can adequately praise the great splendor of the gleanings and gatherings one makes with the words of the prayer?

When speech comes forth it comes from the soul. There is a hint of this in the way the Aramaic Targum translates "and man became a living soul" (Genesis 2:7) — "he became a *speaking* spirit". The utterance comes forth and is heard by the ears — our Rabbis taught that when praying, "You should let your ears hear[10] what you are bringing forth from your mouth" (Berachot 15). Then the utterance begs and

---

10. Let your ears hear. The ears which have to hear the words of the prayers are the ears of the heart (cf. I Kings 3:9). For "true prayer depends on the heart — one has to put oneself in one's prayer with all one's heart, i.e. binding one's thoughts to the words, concentrating on their meaning" (Likutey Moharan I:49,5). Rabbi Nachman said that true devotion in prayer means concentrating on the plain sense of the words you are saying and listening to them very carefully (Rabbi Nachman's Wisdom #75).

pleads with the soul[11] not to leave it behind. As soon as the first letter comes forth — such as the letter Beit of the word Baruch, Blessed (the first word of the Amida prayer), the letter begs and pleads with the soul not to part from it.

The letter says to the soul: "How could you let yourself get separated from me, considering the great bond of love between us? You see my precious beauty, my radiance, my splendor and glory. How could you tear yourself away from me and leave me? True, you have to carry on with the prayer and gather more precious treasures and delights. But how can you separate yourself from me and forget me? At least see to it that whatever place you come to afterwards, you don't forget me or get cut off from me."

All the more so, when one finishes a whole word: the word pleads and entreats in the same manner, caressing and embracing the soul, refusing to let the soul move on. Yet the truth is, one has to go on: there are many more words to be said and many more blessings and prayers to be recited before the conclusion of the service.

The solution is to make the whole prayer into one[12] — to make it into a single unity, so that each individual utterance contains all the utterances making up the whole prayer. From

---

11. The utterance begs and pleads with the soul. In the passage that follows, Rebbe Nachman poetically develops the idea that the person praying should listen to the words he is saying. The Rebbe pictures a dialogue between the letters of the words and the soul of the person praying.

12. Making the whole prayer into one. People on different levels achieve this in different ways. For the great sage and Tzaddik, every single letter, word and section of the prayers has deep mystical significance as part of a single, larger labor of bringing about the unification of the Holy One, blessed-be-He, and the Shechinah. For the simple Jew, the way to make the whole prayer into one is to develop a strong will to attach and devote oneself to God and to put this feeling into every single word of the service (R. Yaakov Meir Shechter).

the beginning of the prayer to the end it should all be one, so that when one reaches the very last word of the prayer one will still be standing at the very first word of the prayer. This way one can pray the entire prayer and still never get separated from even the first letter of the prayer.

The Ultimate Unity

The idea of making a single unity out of the many words and sections of the prayer service helps us to understand the concept of the Tachlis, *the ultimate goal and purpose of life and the creation in general. This is that the absolute unity of God should be perfectly revealed, even in this world of plurality and division. Throughout our time in this world it is most important to keep ourselves constantly aware of the real purpose of life and not let ourselves be deceived by the outward appearance of the world (see Rabbi Nachman's Wisdom #51).*

3. And know that this oneness, this unity, is itself the ultimate goal, the goal of the entire creation. We learn this from the prophecy of Zechariah (14:9): "On that day HaShem will be One and His name One." The prophet speaks of "*that* day" — a future time, when the goal of the creation will have been attained: HaShem will be *One*.

And this ultimate goal is entirely good. For oneness — unity — is entirely good. This we learn from the comment of the Rabbis on this verse in Zechariah: "On that day HaShem will be One and His name One." — "Is this meant to imply," asked the Rabbis, "that right now He is *not* One? Of course not. What it means to say is that in our present state we make a distinction between the different kinds of experiences God sends us in life. When bad things happen, we bless God as 'the true Judge', while when good things happen, we bless Him as 'the good and beneficent'. But in time to come — the time Zechariah was prophesying about — they will bless him for everything as 'the good and beneficent'." (Pesachim 50) Thus we see that unity is the ultimate goal and this goal is entirely good.

Since the ultimate goal is entirely good, in the end everything will turn out to have been for the good. Even when bad things happen and you are beset with troubles and suffering, God forbid, if you look at the ultimate purpose, you will see that these things are not bad at all, they are actually a very great favor. All suffering is sent from God intentionally for your own ultimate good, whether to remind you to return to God, or to cleanse and scour you of your sins. If so, the suffering is really very beneficial, because God's intention is certainly only for good.

Whatever evil and suffering you go through, God forbid, if you will just look at the ultimate goal — God's purpose — you will not experience it as suffering at all. On the contrary, you will be filled with joy at so much good when you look at the purpose of this suffering. Because the ultimate purpose is entirely good, all unity. And the deep truth is, there is no evil at all in the world[13]: everything is good.

Then why do we feel pain when we suffer? The pain people go through because of their suffering is only because their Da'at — divine understanding[14] — is taken from them,

---

13. There is no evil at all in the world. This is not to deny the real evil, pain and suffering so many people experience in life. The point is that in God's scheme of the creation, evil and suffering ultimately serve a good purpose, as the Rabbis commented: " 'And God saw... that it was *very good*' (Genesis 1:31) — this refers to the Angel of Death" (Bereshit Rabbah 9:12).

14. Da'at. Da'at, here translated as "divine understanding", signifies a level of knowledge and awareness that is beyond our everyday consciousness. Da'at — achieved through deep understanding of Torah and the self-purification attained through much prayer — is the knowledge that everything in this

and they are unable to focus on the ultimate purpose, which is entirely good. It is then that they feel the pain and sorrow of their suffering. But when understanding is present and one keeps one's attention on the ultimate goal, one does not feel pain and suffering at all.

The Pain Response

Through this you will be able to understand a deep mystery: why it is a natural reflex response that when someone is going through great pain, God forbid, as for example when having a limb amputated, they screw their eyes up and shut them tight.

We know from experience that when we want to look at a distant object we narrow our eyes and screw them up in order to focus our vision on the object we want to see. Vision is the agent the mind sends to bring the object in question into the brain. We look at something because we want to know what it is. Knowledge is in the mind. When the mind wants to know the nature of an object, it sends forth vision, and the vision goes and views the object and brings it into the mind. The individual then knows what he sees.

This is why, when an object passes by at high speed, we may not know what it is even if we actually saw it with our own eyes. The object passes by so quickly that there is insufficient time to bring the knowledge of it into the brain. And when something is very far away, our power of vision may

world derives from God. In the scheme of the Sefirot, the Sefirah of Da'at is above Chessed, lovingkindness, and Gevurah, power and severity, which are the source of good and evil in this world. Da'at is the root of both Chessed and Gevurah, which are unified there. Thus Da'at-consciousness transcends the everyday consciousness in which some things are experienced as good and others as bad, and with Da'at one can understand that everything is for good.

be inadequate to reach there to bring it back into the brain. We tend to be distracted by the various things we see from the side, and in addition our vision gets diffused over such a great distance — it becomes weakened and lacks sufficient power to bring the object we see into the brain.

This is why we have to narrow our eyes to see a distant object. We have to limit our vision so that other things should not interfere, and we have to focus it on the desired object in order to strengthen our vision and avoid its being diffused. Then it is possible to see the far-off object.

So it is when we want to look at the ultimate goal of Creation, which is all good, all unity. One has to close one's (physical) eyes and focus one's vision — i.e. the inner vision of the soul — on the goal. For the light of this ultimate goal is very far away. The only way to see it is by closing one's eyes. One has to close them completely and keep them firmly shut. One may even have to press on them with one's finger to keep them shut tight. Then one can gaze on this ultimate goal.

In other words, you must turn your eyes away from this world[15] and close them to it completely. You must keep them shut tight, and not look at the vanity of this world and its mundane temptations at all. Then you will be able to see and apprehend the light of the ultimate goal, which is all good. And then the suffering will disappear. For the main reason why one suffers is because one is far from this goal.

That is why it is a natural response[16] to screw up one's eyes when undergoing pain — in order to escape from the suffering and nullify the pain through gazing at the ultimate goal, which is entirely good. For the only way to see this

---

15. **You must turn your eyes away from this world.** For further explanation, see "Insights" #1.

16. **It is a natural response.** See "Insights" #2.

goal is by closing one's eyes. And even though the individual may be totally unaware of what he is doing, the soul knows everything. That is why it is stamped in our nature to close our eyes when going through pain.

Transcendence

> *It is sometimes possible to transcend suffering through finding a Godly purpose in it. But people who have made a genuine effort to do this know that one sometimes experiences transcendence and joyous acceptance for a moment, only to find oneself falling back soon afterwards into a vortex of even more intense pain and suffering. Rebbe Nachman now explains why it is impossible in our present state to experience transcendence more than briefly, vividly depicting the struggles people go through when fighting pain and suffering.*

4. And it really is true that at the moment of bittul[17] — that state of self-transcendence when one becomes nullified in the ultimate goal, which is all good, all unity — at that moment the pain and suffering are nullified and actually disappear. However it is not possible to remain in this state of bittul all the time, because that would be beyond the limitations of our human existence. In this lifetime bittul can only be experienced for limited periods, the way the angels in Ezekiel's prophecy of the Chariot are described as "running and returning" (Ezekiel 1:14). They "run forth", transcending their limitations for a moment, rising towards God, and then they "return" again to their separate selves.

---

17. **Bittul.** The concept of bittul is discussed in the section on "Self-Centered or God-Centered" in "A Matter of Faith" (above). See also "Insights" #3, and "Other Teachings" — "Making Yourself into Nothing".

When a person returns from the state of bittul to normal consciousness, the conscious mind comes back to the brain, which is the seat of the mind, the "vessel" of consciousness. But the limited human brain — the vessel — is unable to hold the transcendent state of bittul, because this is Ein Sof, limitless Infinity — which is the ultimate goal: all one, all good. As a result, the brain now feels the pain of the suffering, because it is in the brain that all sensations of pain and suffering are felt. Nerve passages extend from the brain to all the limbs in the body, and through them the brain is aware of pain in whatever limb it may be.

And know that afterwards, when one returns from the state of bittul back to the "vessels", namely normal consciousness, the pain and suffering attack even more strongly than before. It is like two fighters wrestling with one another: when one of them sees that the other is getting the upper hand he fights back even harder. Similarly, when the forces of judgement gripping a person see that he wants to overcome his suffering and nullify it through bittul, absorption in the ultimate goal, they attack even more strongly. This is why afterwards, when one returns from the state of bittul, the suffering is felt even more intensely than before[18], because the forces of judgement fight back against him since he wanted to escape from them.

Consolation

Afterwards, however, the suffering is lightened and we can derive a measure of consolation[19] from the new spiritual insights we achieve as a result of the suffering. The reason why suffering leads to spiritual insight is that suffering brings one to bittul. Then afterwards, even though one returns from bittul

18. **The suffering is felt even more intensely than before.** See "Insights" #4.

19. **Consolation.** See "Insights" #5 and #6.

to normal consciousness, a trace of the bittul still remains, and from this trace comes Torah insight. The reason for this is that while in the state of bittul, when nullified in the ultimate goal, one realizes that one's pain and suffering are actually of very great benefit. As a result one becomes filled with joy — and joy is the "vessel" for receiving new Torah insight.

This last idea, that we receive Torah insight through joy, is derived from a Rabbinic teaching: "When the Jewish People accepted the Torah with the declaration, 'We will do and we will hear' (Exodus 19:8; 24:7), six hundred thousand angels came down and placed two crowns on the head of each one; and when they sinned with the golden calf, one of the two crowns was removed. But in the future the Holy One blessed-be-He is destined to return the crowns to us, in accordance with the prophecy: 'And eternal joy *on their heads*' (Isaiah 35:10)" (Shabbos 88.) The crowns that were, and will be "on their heads" are the reward for the declaration of "We will do and we will hear" with which the Jews received the Torah. Since the prophecy associates these crowns with joy — 'eternal joy on their heads' — clearly joy is an integral part of the concept of "We will do and we will hear", and therefore bound up with receiving the Torah.

It is the deepening of Torah insight resulting from the remaining joyous trace of the bittul that later cools the intensity of one's suffering. For Torah quenches the thirst of the soul, namely the experience of pain and suffering. Salt makes one thirsty and is thus symbolic of suffering. The Rabbis associated salt with suffering when they said, "The Covenant is mentioned in relation to salt (Leviticus 2:13), and it is mentioned in relation to suffering (Deuteronomy 28:69)" (Berachot 5).

Why does the soul become thirsty? The soul is the daughter of the divine intellect within us. The divine intellect nurtures and cultivates the soul until it develops it to perfection, as it is written, "Without wisdom the soul is not good"

(Proverbs 19:2) — implying that the soul is only good when the individual possesses wisdom — divine intellect. When the divine intellect is fully developed, it produces fruits. But when the divine intellect in a person is spoiled, the "fertile land turns into a salty waste"[20] (Psalms 107:34). This saltiness is the suffering one goes through because one's divine intellect is inadequately developed. This is the thirst of the soul. But through the enhancement of one's understanding of Torah, through deepened spiritual insight, the suffering is cooled and the thirst is quenched: "Ho, all who are thirsty, come to water!" (Isaiah 55:1).

"Happy is the man whom God chastises and from Your Torah you teach him." (Psalms 94:12) The chastisement — the suffering — is what brings one to greater Torah insight. And indeed, if out of suffering you come to enhanced understanding, this is a sign that you have accomplished something and that you dealt with the suffering in the proper way. Your deepened spiritual awareness is a sign that you were able to use the suffering to attain the state of bittul, nullification in the ultimate goal, because the trace that remains after the state of bittul is what gives rise to the enhanced Torah understanding.

Allusions

Rebbe Nachman now returns to the theme of how the Master of the Field works to fix all the souls by bringing them to perfect prayer. He shows that this idea is alluded to in a statement of the Rabbis (Shabbat 104a)

---

20. fertile land... salty waste. Rebbe Nachman's reference to this verse points up the thematic relationship between this section and the idea of the Field of the Souls with which the lesson opens. The ideal is for the souls to produce "fruits" — mitzvot and good deeds.

about the five Hebrew letters Mem, Nun, Tsaddi, Phe and Chaf, which are written differently depending on whether they are in the beginning and middle or at the end of a word.

When the eyes of the Master of the Field shine and the field is the "field of visionaries", he can look into each soul and see if it is near to the ultimate goal. And when he sees that someone is far from the goal, the sign is that this person's prayer is not yet perfected and complete, for he is still unable to make the whole prayer into a unity: when he gets to the end of a word he has forgotten the beginning of the word. Then the Master of the Field looks into him and brings him to the goal, which is all one, all unity. Then he is able to make a unity of the entire prayer, and even when he stands at the end of the prayer, he is still standing at the beginning of the very first word.

This is the idea of the Rabbinic saying that "The visionaries said MaNTsPhaCh" (Shabbat 104a). The reference is to the five letters of the Hebrew alphabet which are written differently when they appear at the end of a word from the way they are written at the beginning or in the middle of a word. The five letters are Mem, Nun, Tsaddi, Phe and Chaf — MaNTsPhaCH.

The Talmud tells us that "the visionaries fixed the one that is at the beginning of the word and the one that is at the end of the word." The words of the Talmud can be understood allusively. The concept of the visionaries is the same as that of the Master of the Field. When his eyes shine and the field is the "field of the visionaries", he is able to "fix the one that is at the beginning of the word and the one that is at the end of the word". In other words, he can look at and fix those who are close to the ultimate goal, and when they stand at the end of the prayer they are still at the beginning of the word — the opening word of the prayer.

And he can also look at and fix those who are far from the goal. They are called "the end of the word", for when they are at the end of the word, they are literally at the end of the word — they have forgotten the beginning. And the visionaries fix them and put them right and bring them to the goal. The Talmud alludes to this as well, stating that "they forgot them, and they went back and fixed them again". On the literal plane the Talmud is telling us that in the course of time the five letters of MaNTsPhaCh were forgotten, and had to be reinstituted. But the Talmud is also alluding to the souls which, because of their distance from the ultimate goal, forget the beginning of the word, since they fail to make their prayer into a unity. "And they [the visionaries] went back and fixed them again" — so that their prayer should be all one, as explained above.

"And Bo'az said to Ruth..."

> "And Bo'az said to Ruth, 'Please listen, my daughter, don't go to glean in someone else's field, and also don't pass on from here... Keep your eyes on the field where they are reaping, and go behind them. I've told the young men not to touch you. If you are thirsty, go to the vessels and drink from what the young men have drawn.' "
>
> (Ruth 2:8-9)

5. All the above teachings are contained in these verses:

And Bo'az said to Ruth: Boaz represents the divine intellect, the sechel, as it is written "Wisdom will give strength ('oz) to the wise" (Ecclesiastes 7:19). Ruth represents the soul, the nefesh, which is the source of all our words of prayer, song and praise. The Rabbis hinted at this when they said "Why was her name called Ruth? Because from her came David, who satiated (Heb. RiVaH) the Holy One with songs and praises" (Berachot 7b).

Please listen, my daughter: He calls her his daughter, because the soul is the daughter of the divine intellect, as we saw above. The intellect tells the soul to listen — to listen to the words of the prayer, as in the Rabbinic dictum quoted above: "You should let your ears hear what you are bringing forth from your mouth" (Berachot 15). Listen carefully and hear what the words are saying, hear each one pleading, "Don't tear yourself away, don't leave me behind."

This is the allusion in the words, **don't go to glean in someone else's field.** For all the letters and words of the prayers are precious bundles gathered from the supernal fields. And each word pleads with the soul not to leave it behind and go off to collect other bundles. But this would be impossible. You have to go forward to collect more — you have to continue with the rest of the prayers.

And also don't pass on from here — in other words, even if you go on to another word, do not pass away from the first word. The only way to do this is to achieve the ultimate goal, as discussed above. And this idea is alluded to in the words that follow:

Keep your eyes on the field where they are reaping. One must focus on the ultimate goal — reaping symbolizes the ultimate goal of creation, because reaping is the goal of ploughing and sowing.

I've told the young men not to touch you. These words hint at the idea of closing one's eyes — for one has to shut them tight in order to focus on the ultimate goal. Without doing this it is impossible to see the goal. The Hebrew for "I've told" is TZiViSi — an expression which also has the connotation of attaching and joining[21]. One has to join and bind one's vision to the goal, shutting the eyes tightly to the vanities of this world. The eyes are called "young men" — because they

---

21. **Attaching and joining.** See "Insights" #7.

are the attendants of the divine intellect. Vision is the agent and emissary of the intellect, as discussed above.

...not to touch you (Heb. nig'ech) This alludes to the afflictions (niga'im) of the soul — for when one's vision is dissipated and one is distracted by all the things in front of one — when one fails to close one's eyes tightly so as not to look at this world — the soul is afflicted. One has to "instruct the young men" — i.e. to close the eyes tight, so as not to look at the vanities of this world even out of the corner of one's eye, in order not to afflict the soul. Then one can look upon the ultimate goal. And through gazing upon the ultimate goal, all the suffering disappears, as explained above.

However, afterwards, when one returns from the state of bittul, the suffering is felt even more intensely than before. This is because of the thirst of the soul. And then: **if you are thirsty, go to the vessels and drink from what the young men have drawn.** For the way to quench the thirst of the soul is through attaining new Torah insights. We get them from the brain, the vessel of the intellect, through the trace which remains after the experience of bittul. It is from here that the soul drinks to quench its thirst. **Drink from what the young men have drawn** — for the young men — the eyes of the intellect — draw new Torah insights from the trace which is left after gazing at the ultimate goal. Through this the suffering afterwards disappears and the thirst of the soul is quenched.

Hope

The essential theme of the whole lesson has been the Tachlis, the ultimate goal of our lives and the world. Rebbe Nachman concludes the lesson on a note of hope, looking forward to the fulfilment of this goal in the Messianic future. God will make a dance-circle of the

Tzaddikim and each one will point with his finger, "This is HaShem — we waited for him". The hopes of the Tzaddikim will then be fulfilled, because in the end it will be seen that all the trials and troubles of this world were sent only to prepare the way for this goal.

Rabbi Elazar said: "In time to come, the Holy One blessed-be-He will make a dance-circle of the Tzaddikim. He will sit in their midst in the Garden of Eden, and each one will point with his finger, as prophesied, 'On that day it will be said, This is our God — we waited for Him and He saved us; this is HaShem — we waited for Him. We will be happy and rejoice over His salvation' (Isaiah 25:9)" (Ta'anit 31a.)

The Garden of the Souls is the Garden of Eden[22], represented in the figures of Moses and Aaron. The Garden is the soul — as in the verse "and their soul shall be like a watered garden" (Jeremiah 31:12). Eden is the ultimate goal of the Creation, for "Eden no eye has seen" (Berachot 34b). No eye has seen Eden because the ultimate goal can only be apprehended through bittul — self-transcendence. (An eye seeing something implies a separation between subject and object. Since the ultimate goal is absolute unity, it can only be apprehended when the subjective eye, the self is no longer separate but transcended and merged in the goal. Therefore "No eye has seen it".)

The Talmud tells us: "In time to come, the Holy One blessed-be-He will make a dance-circle of the Tzaddikim. He will sit in their midst in the Garden of Eden, and each one will point with his finger, etc." (Ta'anit 31). The dance-circle[23] symbolizes Simchah, joy — this is the "vessel" with

---

22. **The Garden of Eden.** See "Insights" #8.

23. **The dance-circle.** A dance circle has no beginning or end, so no-one is first or last, everyone is equal. This symbolizes the harmony that will

which we receive Torah. After the state of bittul, a residue of the bittul remains and shines within us: this trace is the source of new Torah insight, as explained above. This is expressed in the idea that each of the Tzaddikim "points with his finger". The Hebrew for "points" is mar'eh — literally "shows", alluding to the shining residue of the bittul from which new Torah insight comes. Each Tzaddik "points with his finger"[24]. — the finger is an allusion to the Torah which was inscribed with "finger of God" (Exodus 31:18).

prevail in the future: no-one will have any reason to hate or be jealous of anyone else (Bnei Yisoschor Ma'amarei Chodshei Tamuz-Av 4:1).

24. Each Tzaddik "points with his finger". See "Insights" #9.

5

INSIGHTS

At Rebbe Nachman's request, Rabbi Nathan composed "Likutey Halachot", an eight-volume work in which the laws of the Shulchan Aruch — the standard legal compendium governing the life of the Jew — are explained in the light of ideas in Likutey Moharan. Likutey Halachot is not strictly speaking a commentary on Likutey Moharan. However Rabbi Nathan's treatment of the ideas in Rebbe Nachman's lessons throws much light on their interpretation and wider implications.

The following extracts are drawn from Rabbi Nathan's discussions based on the teaching of "Garden of the Souls" in Likutey Moharan I:65. They have been translated from "Torat Nathan", a digest of the comments in "Likutey Halachot" relating to each lesson in Likutey Moharan, edited by R. Noson Zvi Koenig (Kolel Breslov, Bnei Brak).

1. Only through closing our eyes completely to this world and looking at the ultimate, eternal purpose can we nullify all suffering and come to perfect prayer.

The Rabbis taught us to say, "Everything the Loving One does is for good". But if everything God does to a person is for their own good, and if pain and suffering are great favors helping to bring one to eternal life, then why are we commanded to pray about trouble?

Certainly everything God does to a person is all for good, but even so one still has to pray to God and beg Him for relief from suffering. To understand why, we must first recognize that the main purpose of the creation of the world was for the sake of man, who is endowed with free will. God put everything into our hands so that *we* should be the ones to make vessels through which Divine love and blessing can flow into the world.

A vessel is a container used to hold something and pass it to someone else. In Kabbalistic literature, Torah teachings, prayers, mitzvot and good deeds are called vessels — finite channels through which the infinite light of God can be revealed in this world. Until we prepare the appropriate vessels down below, Divine kindness cannot flow to us from above, because if it did it would come down in excess — just as too much oil puts out the lamp. Kindness would then turn into harsh judgement, God forbid.

The vessels for receiving God's kindness are prepared through Torah study and prayer, especially prayer. Thus before the creation of man, "no shrub of the field was yet in the earth, and no herb of the field had yet sprung up, for God had not caused it to rain upon the earth and there was no man to work the land" (Genesis 2:5). Rashi (ad loc.) explains that man was not yet there to pray — his prayer was needed to initiate the flow of divine blessing.

Therefore before a person prays, everything that comes to him, even the suffering, is all for his good. The very suffering he goes through is actually an expression of great love by God, because, given his unholy behavior, there is no other way for blessing and life to come down to him at this stage in his development. If he were blessed with pure kindness without limitation, the light would be excessive and it would do more harm than good.

Through prayer we sweeten the Divine judgements that restrict the flow of kindness, and prepare the vessels through which we can then receive God's kindness. We are then able to nullify the harsh judgements, since we now have the vessels with which to receive God's infinite kindness and goodness without having to go through suffering.

In order to prepare the vessels, the first stage is to lift our eyes to the ultimate goal, where everything is good, and to make a unity out of all our prayers. It is only by surrendering ourselves in bittul to the ultimate unity, knowing and believing that everything is for good, that we can afterwards pray for all the things we need. The reason is because the vessels with which we receive God's abundant blessings — children, health, wealth, etc. — are actually formed from the light of the trace of the bittul-experience that remains after returning to normal consciousness. Having prepared the appropriate vessels with which to receive God's blessing and kindness, everything is now for good.

This is the meaning of Rebbe Nachman's saying that after returning from bittul, we quench the thirst of the soul caused by suffering through the Torah we receive from the trace. This Torah actually comes to us through prayer. This is a point the Rebbe makes in many places — cf. Likutey Moharan I:8 and I:19 — and it is evident here too. The Rebbe first speaks about how to make one out of all the prayers through contemplating the ultimate goal, and then concludes that through contemplating the ultimate goal we draw down Torah from the trace. Clearly the Torah insight comes down to us through prayer.

The fact is that prayer and Torah insight are dependent on each other. It is through prayer that we first connect ourselves to the radiance of the trace. This is how we draw down the wellsprings of light that later expand within us in the form of the deepened Torah insight with which we cool and temper our suffering. This is because it is through prayer and Torah that we form the vessels with which we receive the influx of God's blessing — for goodness, eternity and *life* rather than for evil and death.

Only through the true Tzaddikim can we learn how to pray. Accordingly the Rabbis said that anyone who has a sick person at home should go to the Sage (Baba Batra 116a). The reason is that only the true Tzaddik — the Master of the Field mentioned in the lesson — knows how to look into the soul of each one and sees how far he is from the ultimate goal, to what extent his prayer is still not merged in unity, and what is needed in order to bring him to the ultimate goal.

2. It is a natural reflex response that when someone is going through great pain... they shut their eyes firmly.

Closing one's eyes in pain is only one aspect of bittul and only temporary. To be worthy of attaining true bittul through suffering takes great merit. The Rebbe indicates this when he states later that enhanced Torah insight is a sign that one has dealt with one's suffering in the proper way. From this it is clear that not everyone attains complete bittul through their suffering, only the Tzaddikim and other pure individuals. One needs to be very strong and persistent and beg God to help one surrender oneself to Him through one's suffering.

3. Bittul

There is no possible way of escaping the troubles that pass over the Jewish People collectively or each Jew individually except through surrender to the Tachlis — i.e. closing one's eyes firmly and acting as if one is asleep, nullifying oneself completely as if one has no feelings and sensations whatsover, attaching and surrendering one's thoughts to the light of the Infinite.

I heard the Rebbe say that this is something everyone is capable of doing. Even if one is unable to achieve perfect bittul in the way of the great Tzaddikim, everyone has the ability to nullify themselves for a time if they really want to, and can thereby transcend all pain and suffering. It could be that afterwards the pain and suffering will attack again. Then one has to fight them through developing new Torah ideas, or through throwing oneself into Torah study with renewed vigor.

4. Bittul in the mode of "running and returning", and the dawning awareness that comes from bittul.

A point that everyone should be aware of is that any time some new awareness of God begins to dawn on them or they experience a new spiritual awakening, they immediately become subject to even stronger attacks from the forces of judgement — in the form of attacks of material desires, inner confusion, outside distractions, etc. You must be very strong and not allow yourself to fall down as a result. Don't let yourself be discouraged even if you find yourself subject to these attacks time and time again. The way to keep yourself strong is through Torah. If you are not able to develop original Torah ideas, then at least make every endeavor to put fresh effort into your Torah study, and follow the Torah path in all its details simply and sincerely. Don't go aside from the Torah path in any way.

The light and fire of devotion you feel as a result of bittul may make you feel you want to be very holy and to separate yourself completely from the vanity of this world — and certainly this is the ideal. But be aware that this is the moment the evil inclination attacks more strongly than ever. Don't let yourself fall down, and don't get discouraged. Just keep strong and don't stray from the Torah path. "Don't be over saintly... Don't be excessively wicked" (Ecclesiastes 7:16-17). I.e. one should not allow oneself to fall into evil as a result of being spiritually over-ambitious — trying being extremely saintly but failing.

If you follow this advice and keep your determination up, you will make sure, steady progress and you will always be able to inspire yourself and keep away from the vanities of the world and lift yourself up to God. If you are able to genuinely surrender yourself and close your eyes to the world, well and good. If not, in any event don't let yourself fall down because you feel you aren't succeeding. Just keep following the Torah path simply as best as you can.

5. It really is true that at the moment of bittul the pain and suffering are nullified and actually disappear.

The most important part of sweetening the pain and suffering is not through the state of bittul itself but through the deeper Torah insight that comes from the trace of higher consciousness that remains after the bittul.

It is true that during the actual moment of bittul and surrender to the Tachlis, pain and suffering are transcended completely, because on that level the harsh judgements have no hold at all. But this still does not sweeten the pain and suffering on the level of normal consciousness, which is where they have their real hold. This is why when one comes out of the state of bittul, they attack more strongly than ever. The forces of judgement gripping one see that one is trying to overcome one's suffering and nullify it through bittul. They therefore attack even more strongly, like when two fighters are wrestling and one sees that the other is getting the upper hand: he fights back even harder.

This is the time to overcome the harsh judgements through the Torah one draws from the trace that remains after bittul. The pain and suffering are sweetened in the very place where they have their hold, and this is the most important part of the process.

6. Bittul to the Tachlis, etc. The renewal of Torah.

Notwithstanding the importance of bittul — surrendering to the Tachlis, which is all unity, and merging all the words of the prayers into one — nevertheless, true perfection comes only when one is able to return from bittul to normal life and draw Godly light into this finite world in a measured way so as to "repair the vessels". For "You have desired praise from creatures made of dust" (from the High Holiday Musaf) — God wants us to serve Him within the very limitations of our condition as humans. This is bound up with the idea of the new Torah insights that come after bittul. The Torah itself is made up of limited vessels — chapters, paragraphs, verses, words and letters etc. One has to draw down the light in a measured way in order that the vessels should be able to hold it and not break because of excessive light.

7. The light of the trace of the bittul

We have to work on carrying out the practical mitzvot in order to be able to receive the light of the trace which remains after bittul and not forget the experience completely. The mitzvot are the vessels through which we receive the light.

The inner soul of every Jew constantly burns with longing for HaShem, because it is in the ultimate goal of Divine unity that the soul itself is rooted, and the soul yearns to be attached and merged with this light. But in our finite state in this world it is only possible to achieve transcendence and bittul for brief moments, "running and returning". When we return from bittul to normal consciousness, the finite mind does not have the vessels to hold the infinite light, and the experience usually passes and is just forgotten.

Moreover, the Evil Inclination in its various manifestations attacks the Jews more than anyone, knowing that the Jew is constantly yearning to escape to the ultimate goal. The saintly Torah scholars long for this goal more than anyone, and are therefore attacked more than anyone (Succah 52a). There are innumerable variations in the way different people experience bittul and strive for the ultimate goal — the experience can even be different for one and the same person at different times and stages of life.

The essential idea underlying the concept of a mitzva is connection — the word mitzva is related to the Hebrew word *tzavta* which means joining and connection. Each of the different mitzvot is a way of attaching the light of the trace left after bittul to the finite mind: this is how we become attached to God. Conversely the Hebrew word *'avera*, which means a sin, comes from the word *'avar*, which means gone, passed away, because through a sin the light of the trace passes and goes from a person. This is why "one mitzva leads to another and one sin leads to another" (Avot 4:2) — because each time we do a mitzva we bind the light of the trace to ourselves and thus become attached to HaShem, causing the light of other mitzvot — all of which are rooted there — to shine down to us. The converse applies to sins. It is thus through the Torah and the mitzvot — which are drawn from the trace of the bittul — that the Jewish People become merged in the light of the Infinite.

Everyone has free will, and everyone is able to draw this light on himself. The light of the Infinite radiates even on the lowest, most material levels, because God's light is never cut off. The Kabbalistic writings thus teach that the Kav, the line of light drawn down from the Infinite, shines even in the coarsest materialism — it is just that it is very thickly veiled there. Even so, everyone is capable of attaching themselves to God if they really want to, no matter where they are and what their level. It is purely a matter of willpower, determination and effort. Even in the most intense darkness, in the valley of death itself, one can still draw the light of the Infinite on himself if he will just close his eyes and make himself into nothing for a time. Understand this well — and the main thing is to practice it.

8. The Garden of Eden

Eden is the concept of bittul to the ultimate goal. Of Eden it is written, "No eye has seen it" (Isaiah 64:3). This is the concept of bittul. No eye has seen it — because the "experience" of Eden is one where self is transcended. There is no longer a separation between the observer — the viewing eye — and the object observed. There is no eye! A trace of this light remains after bittul — this trace is expressed in the concept of the Garden, a place of the greatest purity and translucence, where it is possible to receive a radiation from the light of bittul, Eden. The Garden of Eden is the holy field mentioned at the beginning of the lesson, where the souls grow. The concept with which the lesson starts is thus closely related to the later explanation of the concept of bittul.

The Garden of Eden is the field "which HaShem has blessed" (Genesis 27:27 — see Zohar I:128). The purpose of healing and fixing the souls in the field is so that they should be able to be merged in the light of the Infinite and take delight in HaShem. This *is* the delight of the World to Come, the Garden of Eden, the world of the souls.

Prior to Adam's sin he was able to attain this delight while alive in this world. God put him in the Garden "to work it and guard it" (Genesis 2:15) — to work it, i.e. to fulfil the positive commandments, and to guard it, i.e. through observing the negative commandments (Zohar I:27). In other words Adam only had to observe the Torah in order to become merged with the Infinite and enjoy the light without any need for the light to be dimmed and coarsened.

As a result of the sin, however, "Man cannot abide in honor" (Psalm 49:13). He was driven out of the Garden of Eden and God positioned the cherubim and the blade of the flaming sword that turned every way in order to guard the way to the tree of life (Genesis 3:24). The cherubim and the sword are the forces which keep pushing us back from experiencing the Infinite light — which is the source of eternal life. One is constantly confused and distracted by temptations etc. Our inability to settle our minds is expressed in the idea of the blade of the sword turning every way.

Today it takes much effort before one can become merged with the light, and it is only possible to receive the light through many garments and vessels. These are the "clothes of skins" that Adam and Eve wore after the expulsion from Eden (Genesis 3:21). The Infinite light itself is way beyond our ablity to apprehend — only when the light is dimmed and contracted and veiled in many garments — the vessels — can we begin to perceive it. This is why our main task in this life is to prepare the right vessels to receive the light.

9. Each Tzaddik "points with his finger" — the finger is an allusion to the Torah which was inscribed with "finger of God".

The Torah we receive after bittul protects our eyes against an attack from the unholy forces. They fall in face of the Torah. "HaShem's commandment is pure, lighting up the eyes" (Psalms 19:9). When the Tzaddikim return from bittul and open their eyes, they do not look at the vanity of this world: they guard their eyes with the Torah they received from the trace remaining after bittul, and through this all harsh judgements and suffering are done away with.

6

OTHER TEACHINGS

Faith

Rebbe Nachman said that those who try to find the meaning of existence through science and philosophy have no life, even in this world. As soon as things go against them, they are left with nothing. They depend completely on nature and have nowhere to turn. When trouble strikes, they are left without any source of inspiration.

But someone who has faith in God has a very good life. Even in times of trouble, his faith still inspires him. He trusts in God and knows that everything will be for the best. Even if he has to go through suffering, he realizes it will atone for his sins. And if this is not necessary, these troubles will ultimately bring him a much greater benefit. No matter what happens, he realizes that God ultimately only does good. Someone with faith therefore always has a good life, both in this world and the next.

However the people who try to find the meaning of existence through science and philosophy have no life either in this world or the next. It is well known that their lives are always filled with suffering. No matter what happens, things never seem to go their way. Actually, it is impossible that they should, because these people have chosen this world, which is a realm of suffering and trouble. All their chosen world has to offer them is pain and worry.

This world never gives a person everything he desires. Someone who ignores his true purpose and seeks worldly pleasure will only find a world filled with suffering. He will constantly encounter trouble and anxiety, and through it all, will have nothing to console him.

If you have faith, you have hope in the World to Come. You therefore have a very good life, because you know that everything is for good, even your suffering. Suffering comes either to remind you to repent or to atone for your sins. Ultimately, it will allow you to attain the everlasting good of the World to Come.

Your faith itself may cause you to suffer: it could be that the sins and other wrongs you have committed cause you great anguish. You may suffer the greatest agonies of regret. Still, this is for your good. It is written, "The fear of God increases one's days" (Prov.10:27). The agony of regret is not bad, because it increases your days and adds to your life.

But troubles and anxieties shorten and destroy people's lives. Those who reject faith in God therefore have no life, because their troubles and anxieties completely destroy their lives. But "the fear of God increases one's days." When a person's troubles and anxieties stem from their fear of God, they actually add to their life.

You may have great pain when you regret your sins. You may contemplate God's greatness and cringe because of your wrongdoings. Or you may recall that God punishes, and tremble with anxiety. In either case, your suffering comes from your fear of God and is included in the verse, "The fear of God increases one's days." This is the suffering and anxiety that adds to your life.

Rabbi Nachman's Wisdom #102

The Problem Contains Its Own Solution

"Ba-tzar hirchavta li" — "In my distress you relieved me."
(Psalms 4:2)

Even in times of trouble, God sends what He sends in such a way that the trouble itself contains the salvation. Keep your eyes open for God's love and mercy! If you look carefully you will see that even when God sends you trouble, He still helps you even when you're right in it. He actually helps you by means of the very problem itself, treating you with tremendous kindness all along.

This is the meaning of King David's words: "Ba-tzar hirchavta li" — "In my distress you relieved me" (Psalms 4:2). In and by means of the very trouble itself You have helped me! Of course we would like our troubles to be over, and we confidently expect that God will soon save us from all of them and benefit us greatly. Yet even now, while our troubles are still with us, God is helping us.

Likutey Moharan I:195

Show Us A Love That *We* Understand

When the sons of Jacob were about to journey to Egypt with Benjamin, Jacob said to them, "May the eternal God *give you love*". This expresses the very essence of Godly love, when He gives *you* the love — i.e. when God puts His love in *our* hands. For God, it could be that even serious illness and other forms of suffering are expressions of His love, because certainly everything God does to a person He does out of love, even when He sends them severe pain and suffering. But we ask that He should entrust His love to us and put it in *our* hands, because we do not understand His love and we are unable to bear it.

May God just put the love into *our* hands and give us love in our terms, because we understand love in the simple sense where it means healing from disease and so on.

Likutey Moharan II:62

Accepting the Bad Things

"Love your fellow (RE'ACha) like yourself, I am God."
(Leviticus 19:18)

One of the teachings that comes out of this verse is that you should accept all the bad things and suffering you go through in your life with love. You have to understand that, considering all the wrong you have done in your life, God is actually treating you very mercifully and sending you less suffering than you really deserve. If God were to give you the full punishment for what you have done, you would have to suffer much more, God forbid.

The Hebrew words "Ve-ahavta le-Re'ACha kamocha" — "love your neighbor" — can be read "Ve-ahavta le-*Ra*'ACha...", meaning "love your bad..." — i.e. accept your suffering and all the bad things which happen to you with love. Because "...like yourself!" — i.e. considering the way you are and considering all your bad deeds, "I am God" — "I am full of compassion and I am still treating you with great mercy."

Likutey Moharan I:165

Abraham, Isaac and Jacob:
Sweetening the Harsh Judgements

Each person must work to heal his soul — the nefesh. This means raising it up to the place where it is rooted, which is done by laboring hard at one's Torah study until one knows and understands the Torah.

As one goes through life, the different situations one finds oneself in are all sent from Heaven. They are Divine "judgements". There are two main kinds of judgements. One is those sent to people through unholy agents — the prototype is the serpent that "cast impurity upon Eve" (Shabbat 146).

The other category is the Holy Judgement, through which "God disciplines someone He loves" (Proverbs 3:12).

An example of this latter kind is when a person starts making a new effort in Torah and spiritual devotion, only to find himself frustrated by all kinds of obstacles, whether external or internal. It seems as though all one's efforts are being rejected. But in fact this apparent rejection is really the first stage of being brought nearer to God, and in this sense it is a Holy Judgement.

Why this happens can be explained with reference to the teaching of the Rabbis (Ta'anit 8): "Everyone who sets himself right down below is judged righteously in the judgement above". When a person tries to "set himself right" and draw close to God, he is "judged righteously" — that is to say, he is treated severely. The suffering he goes through seems like rejection, as if everything is conspiring to push him off the path of devotion, God forbid. But the truth is that this severe treatment is designed to draw him closer, and is for his own ultimate good, because "God disciplines someone He loves". The intention is that he should stand up to the test and thereby get stronger and make even greater efforts to come closer.

Accordingly, when a person wants to achieve something holy, obstacles are sent to him to increase his determination to accomplish what he wants (cf. Likutey Moharan I:66). This is why this kind of "judgement" is a Holy Judgement. Only it is hard for the person going through it to understand this at the time, because the very experience itself puts him into a state of constricted consciousness. At that moment he lacks the higher insight necessary to understand the real significance of what he is going through.

The idea of Holy Judgement is expressed in the idea that "Abraham gave birth to Isaac" (Genesis 25:19). Abraham symbolizes lovingkindness, while Isaac symbolizes sternness — his way of approaching the Almighty was primarily with awe, "the Fear of Isaac" (Genesis 31:53). When the Torah tells us that "Abraham gave birth to Isaac", it means that the Holy Judgement, symbolized in Isaac, is born from — derives from — Abraham, lovingkindness. The apparently harsh judgement is really a garb for great lovingkindness, because it is sent for the person's long-term benefit: "God disciplines someone He loves." The ultimate purpose of our hardships and difficulties is to bring us closer to God.

Nevertheless we have to see to it to sweeten the harsh judgements, because they stem from constricted consciousness, and our task in life is to rise from constricted to expanded consciousness. It is when one is in a state of constricted consciousness that one feels the full severity of judgement. The individual is in a state of spiritual darkness, and so too Isaac's "eyes were dimmed from seeing" (Genesis 27:1) Darkness is associated with night-time — "And the darkness He called night" (Genesis 1:5).

The nefesh-level of the soul is also a concept of night — "with my soul [nefesh] I have longed for you in the night" (Isaiah 26:9). The nefesh is "night" as compared to the higher levels of the soul, which radiate more brightly. One has to see to it to go from constricted consciousness to expanded consciousness, thereby sweetening the Judgement. Expanded consciousness is a state of enhanced spiritual vision and understanding — "their eyes were opened" (Genesis 3:7). Rashi (ad loc.) explains that this refers to wisdom, because the essential element in sweetening the Judgement is wisdom, namely Torah knowledge. The Torah is light (Proverbs 6:23). Judgement is darkness. The antidote is the light of the Torah, which sweetens the judgement.

The way a person can know if he is subject to a Holy or Unholy Judgement is from his prayers. When one is able to concentrate on his prayers even during difficult times, this is a sign that the Judgement is Holy. Thus the Rabbis taught (Berachot 5a): "Which afflictions stem from God's love? Those which do not interfere with one's prayers, as it is written

(Psalms 66:20): 'Blessed is God who has not turned aside my prayer nor His lovingkindness from me'." Similarly it is written: "You hid Your face, I was shaken" (Psalms 30:8). The "face" is prayer ("Hezekiah turned his *face*... and prayed" — Isaiah 38:2). In other words, when the "face" is hidden and one's prayers are confused, it is a time of hard judgement, God forbid: "I was shaken".

Holy Judgement, on the other hand, derives from Isaac, and "Abraham gave birth to Isaac" — Holy Judgement comes from God's lovingkindness. Rashi comments on the verse "Abraham gave birth to Isaac" (Genesis 25:19): "The Torah testifies that it was Abraham who fathered Isaac because the cynics of the time were saying that Sarah had conceived from Avimelech..." Avimelech symbolizes unholiness. In other words, people may think that the Judgement of Isaac, who was born from Sarah, came from the unholy side — Avimelech — God forbid. "...and therefore God made Isaac's face similar to Abraham's, and everyone acknowledged that Abraham was the father of Isaac." In the state of constricted consciousness it may be hard to understand that the Judgement is an expression of God's love, but this is really the truth. The sign by which one can know is the "face" — i.e. one's prayers. If one is able to concentrate on them properly, this is a sign that the hardship one faces is an expression of God's love.

The way to sweeten the judgement of Isaac is through Wisdom, i.e. Torah knowledge. This is symbolized in the figure of Jacob, who was born from Isaac. Isaac, the nefesh level of the soul, gives birth to two categories — Jacob and Esau. Jacob stands for Wisdom, whereas Esau represents the evil aspect of Judgement, which is sent into the world "when a soul sins" (Leviticus 5:1). Esau said of Jacob, "He has outwitted me (va-Ya'AKVeny)" (Genesis 27:36), which Onkelos translates to mean, "He was wiser than me". This shows that Jacob embodies wisdom. It is only through wisdom, Jacob, that the soul can be healed. It is written of Jacob that "The sun shone upon him" (Genesis 32:32). The sun is "the sun of righteousness, with healing in its wings". (Malachi 3:20).

"God's Torah is whole, restoring the soul" (Psalms 19:8) This means that the wisdom of the Torah, which graces our speech with knowlege and understanding, restores and heals the soul. When a person attains the Wisdom of the Torah, the soul is repaired and elevated to its source. For the drop of seed from which the soul is born originally comes from the brain, the place of Wisdom. This is true not only of the individual, but of the Jewish People as a whole. "Israel arose first in thought" (Bereshit Rabbah 1) i.e. in the Wisdom of the Creator, which is the root of the souls of Israel and of all the worlds. This is the Torah, which is called Wisdom (Proverbs 8:12), and through which the Holy One Blessed-be-He created the worlds (Bereshit Rabbah 1; Zohar I:5a; 134a etc.)

Thus when the soul is lifted up and attains the wisdom of the Torah, all the worlds are renewed and the glory of God is revealed. This is the goal of all our labor.

adapted from Likutey Moharan I:74

Making Yourself Into Nothing

Rabbi Nathan writes:

The Rebbe once told me, "When things are very bad, make yourself into nothing."

I asked him, "How does one make oneself into nothing?"

He replied, "You close your mouth and eyes — and you are like nothing."

We can gain valuable insight from these words. Sometimes you may feel overwhelmed by the Evil Urge. You are very disturbed and confused by evil thoughts, finding it impossible to overcome them. You must then make yourself like nothing.

You no longer exist. Your eyes and your mouth are closed.
Every thought is banished. Your mind ceases to exist. You
have nullified yourself completely before God.

Rabbi Nachman's Wisdom #280

Man is Born to Struggle — Struggle in Torah!

...If there is suffering and trouble in the world, the only
place to escape is to God and His Torah. "For man is born
to struggle" (Job 5:7). On this the Midrash comments, " 'Man
is born to struggle' — happy is the person who struggles with
the Torah."

Whether you are rich or poor, your life will be filled with
struggle and suffering. That is man's lot, as it is written: "For
his days are vexation and pain" (Ecclesiastes 2:23).

In the holy "Sh'nei Luchot HaBrit" (2:138a) we find:

"There is no moment without its torment,
There is no hour that is not sour,
There is no day without dismay..."

Happy is the person who flees from the struggles of this
troublesome world and puts his efforts into the struggle to learn
and understand the Torah. He will be "happy and prosperous"
(Psalms 128:2) — happy in this world, and prosperous in the
future world (Avot 6:4)....

The world was always filled with worries and suffering.
Things have not changed. It is written: "In pain you shall
eat... by the sweat of your brow you shall eat bread" (Genesis
3:17-19). This was decreed from the time of Adam's sin, and
there is nowhere to escape. These worries and pains destroy a
man's life. The only shelter is in God and His Torah.

"This is the way of the Torah," says the Mishnah. "You'll
eat bread with salt, you'll drink water by measure, you'll sleep

on the ground, you'll live a life of discomfort, and you'll toil in the Torah. If you do this, 'You will be happy and prosperous' (Psalms 128:2) — happy in this world and prosperous in the World to Come" (Avot 6:4).

People find this difficult to understand. After telling us the struggles we must endure for the Torah — "you'll eat bread with salt, etc." — how can the Mishnah state "You will be happy...in this world?" Many of the commentators have tried to resolve this homiletically, but their explanations are weak and strained.

But really, there is no question. If you have eyes to see and a heart that truly understands the world, you will know this. If you have absorbed the wisdom contained in the Rebbe's awesome teachings, you know the truth. The Mishnah means exactly what it says.

The wealthiest people in the world will testify that this world is filled with worry and suffering. Rich people suffer as much as everyone else. "The more property, the more worries" (Avot 2:7). Poor people may not realize this. They may think they would no longer have problems if they were rich. But they are sadly mistaken, as we can see with our own eyes. The truth is as our sages have taught it.

Whether you are rich or poor, you cannot avoid worries. The world is filled with pain and suffering and there is no place to escape. If you are a man, you have to worry about earning a living. You are concerned about your wife and children. If you are a woman, you imagine you are troubled by your husband. No matter who you are, you will find that the world abounds with real suffering and pain. How many people suffer because of sickness and accidents? Heaven help us.

There is no escape, except in the Torah.

If you desire the good of this world and want to live at ease without troubles, you will be constantly frustrated. The more you seek the good life, the more you will find the opposite. Everything you manage to grasp will be spoiled because of suffering. Take an honest look and you will see this for yourself.

"There is no wisdom, understanding, or counsel against God" (Proverbs 21:30). The only way to be at ease is to will yourself to subsist on an absolute minimum. Firmly resolve to follow the dictum of the Mishnah: "Eat bread with salt... you will live a life of discomfort..." Be prepared to lead a life of struggle and difficulty in order to involve yourself in the Torah — "...and toil in the Torah."

Only then will you have life, even in this world. "If you do this, you will be happy... in this world." This is certainly true. You will no longer suffer from worldly misfortunes. You have already accepted them upon yourself for the sake of the Torah. All your life — all your good — is the true good. Thus your life is a true life. Happy are you — even in this world.

Someone who wants to live at ease in this world and enjoy its delights will only find bitterness. "Even the slightest breeze will upset him." The smallest mishap will cause him to suffer greatly. You may be immensely rich and powerful. You may be a lord or a king. It is still impossible for everything to be as you desire in a world filled with suffering.... The only way out is to choose the Torah and its commandments. Make up your mind to be satisfied with an absolute minimum in order to immerse yourself in the Torah.

Spend your days with Torah and devotion and you will be immune to the world's travail. You will shake off the toil and struggle of worldly concerns and no longer taste the bitterness of soul they have to offer. Devoted to God and His Torah, you will truly be alive, for this is the root of life, both in this world and the next.

You will then know that the words of the Mishnah are correct, even in their plain meaning. You will have chosen to live such a life, eating bread with salt, drinking water by measure, sleeping on the ground and living a life of discomfort. You must be willing to accept a life of suffering, for there are times when even bread with salt and water by measure will not be abundant. But you accept all this in order to immerse yourself in the Torah — "You will toil in the Torah."

If you do this, you will certainly be "happy and prosperous — happy in this world." You will have accepted all the suffering the world has to offer and you will be worthy of true life. You will then be able to see the truth, and you will know that this world was not created for ease and enjoyment. You will realize that someone who seeks the delights of this world will only find pain and vexation.

The Torah is our life and length of our days. If you flee from the struggle of the world in order to toil in the Torah, you will attain the Future World, which is eternal, and reduces the whole of this world to the wink of an eye in comparison. And besides, you will also have a good life in this world.

The best thing in this world is patience. But this is unattainable without complete immersion in the Torah and its commandments. Open your eyes to the truth and you will see this. Ridicule these words and all you ridicule is yourself. We speak the truth and it is yours to accept. If you wish to turn your back on it and remain immersed in the deep quicksand of this world, no one will stop you...

These were the Rebbe's words to someone who spoke to him at length. The Rebbe knew this man was drowning in endless waters and wanted to rescue him. But the man hardened his heart and turned a stubborn shoulder, not accepting the Rebbe's advice. He knew the Rebbe spoke the truth, but refused to take his words to heart.

The Rebbe said, "He is like a drowning man who is about to die. A rescuer comes along and extends a hand to lift him out of the water. But the drowning man stubbornly moves aside and turns his back in arrogance, not wanting to grasp the helping hand. He tries to get away from the very person who comes to save him."

Heed these words!

You will find pleasure both in this world and the next.

Rabbi Nachman's Wisdom #308

7

PRAYERS

Rebbe Nachman told his followers to "turn the lessons into prayers" (Likutey Moharan II:25) — because the purpose of Torah study is to put the teachings into practice, and the only way to do this is through prayer. Rabbi Nathan wrote extensive prayers based on the lessons in Likutey Moharan. They are collected in his "Likutey Tefilot" — "Collected Prayers". Here are some of Rabbi Nathan's prayers on the theme of suffering. The first is the prayer he wrote on the lesson of "Garden of the Souls".

Likutey Tefilot I:65

Let me close my eyes to this world of distractions!

HaShem! Unified God, Who was, is, and will be:

God of love and kindness. Help me become totally merged in Your unity. Help me to purify myself and fight with all my strength and determination to shut my eyes tight to this world. Let me keep my eyes firmly closed to all the vanities of this world, and pay no attention to them whatsoever. Let me stop getting drawn by material temptations and desires. Let me be just like a blind person as far as this world is concerned, so that my eyes, my thoughts, my intellect, my awareness, and my whole consciousness will be focussed only on the true goal of life, the ultimate, everlasting goal of the entire Creation, until I come to true knowledge of Your real goodness.

Let me understand through and through that ultimately there is no evil in the world at all, that everything is only goodness and lovingkindness, and that You are overflowing with goodness to everyone in the world. For Your intention is only for good. Your whole desire is only to enable us to achieve the true goal of life — eternal life — so that we will have perfect joy at all times.

Help us out of our suffering

Awesome Holy One, please keep me from trouble and suffering. Be with me constantly at all times. And if, Heaven forbid, Your Divine justice and goodness ever require You to send me suffering, help me at the same time by giving me the strength and understanding to look to the ultimate good purpose of the suffering. Let me become completely and genuinely merged with You at the moment of pain. Let me make myself into nothing and shut my eyes to this world and its desires completely, until I can look into the far-off distance and catch sight of the true goal, the eternal goal. Let the suffering bring me to this vision, and with it let all my suffering disappear completely.

Loving God, You know the pain of my heart and my soul. You know how much I have sinned with my eyes — my physical eyes, and the eyes of my intellect. I have looked at things which it is forbidden to look at and I've done terrible damage to my eyes. And all this has caused terrible damage to my soul. I've let the worst thoughts enter my mind, and I've taken myself way outside the bounds of holiness — in all directions. I have delved into matters far above my level while at the same time admitting the lowest thoughts and feelings into my mind. Out of the corner of my eye I have looked way past the boundaries of holiness. And time and time again I have willfully stopped myself thinking of You and Your Holy Torah. I have done this thousands and thousands of times, times without number. Habit has come to be second nature with me.

Save me from my own self!

My mind and my soul are so damaged as a result that I have lost the power of holy speech. I find it impossible to talk to You. I have no idea how to present my prayers to You. And I have still not really repented of these mistakes. I am spiritually so weak that I do not know any way for me to come back to You. I feel so far from You. My mind is so confused. I am hounded from inside and outside — from my own self, and from all my enemies and opponents, both material and spiritual, enemies without number — people of all kinds, Tzaddikim, ordinary people and evil people. "HaShem, how many are my enemies, many are those who rise up against me" (Psalms 3:2).

Take pity on me, pathetic fly that I am. I am so flawed and spoiled. No image would be adequate to depict all my flaws and blemishes, the weakness of my hands, the turbulence of my mind, the pain of my heart, the afflictions of my soul, and the terrible suffering I go through both physically and spiritually.

You warned us to shut our eyes to this world completely, but we have rebelled and gone to the opposite extreme. We have spent our whole time running after the emptiness and vanity of this lowly world. By day we have no rest, and even at night we never stop thinking about worldly things. We have got into the habit of using our minds only to think about making a living and running after the mundane vanities of this world — material gratification, status, and other related desires. We have thrown the real goal of life to the side, and our habits have become so ingrained in us that even when we *want* to think about what is going to happen to us in the end, even when we want to contemplate the real purpose of life, we find it an impossible burden. We cannot concentrate our minds for even a single moment to focus on the real goal. Even when we are trying to study Torah or pray, our thoughts go flying off in every direction, and we are completely distracted by outside concerns.

Where in the world am I?

Where in the world are we? Where is our wisdom? Where is our plain common sense? Where are our minds? What did we come into this lowly world for? To fill our minds with thoughts like these? Didn't we only come into this world to master ourselves and use our free will to break our impulsiveness and turn our minds, our eyes and our hearts away from the mundane world so as to think only of the true goal of life and to bind ourselves to You?

That is what the Torah teaches us again and again: "Don't go astray after your hearts and your eyes, which you lust after" (Numbers 15:39); "Show reverence for HaShem your God, work for Him and be connected to Him, and swear by His name" (Deuteronomy 10:20); "Go after HaShem your God, hold Him in awe, keep His commandments and listen to His voice; work for Him and be connected to Him" (ibid.13:5); "Today I am bringing Heaven and Earth to witness against you: I have put life and death, the blessing and the curse, before you. Choose life, in order that you and your children should live. Love HaShem your God, listen to His voice and attach yourself to Him, because He is your life and the length of your days" (ibid. 30:19-20).

And now, we've turned everything completely upside down. "Does one abandon the waters from the rock in the fields — waters melted from the snow of Lebanon... flowing cold waters" — "...to hew out for themselves broken wells which will not contain water"? (Jeremiah 18:14 and 2:13) Isn't that exactly what we have done? We've turned our thoughts away from the Life of life and from His holy Torah — from the true and eternal Source of life — to think about all the mundane things we dwell on obsessively all day, each person in his own crazy way.

Bring me back before the day of reckoning

Oh God and King! What will we do on the day of judgement? What will we do in the eternal world? How are we to prepare for the day which is wholly Shabbat, the day of ultimate rest, where no one can enter except those who adorn themselves in this world and tear themselves away completely from mundane attachments, binding themselves only to the true and eternal goal of life. And what should we do now that our sins have made us what we are, and "I am sinking in the mud of the deep, where it is impossible to stand, I have come down to the depths of the waters and the swirling torrent has swept me away" (Psalms 69:3).

My father, my father, my father! My God, my God, my God! My King and God, I pray of You, I stretch myself out and prostrate myself before You, I fall before You and plead: for Your own sake only, do what You can in Your overwhelming love and kindness to bring me back to You in perfect Teshuvah, truly and sincerely. From now on, let me live the way I should. From now on help me, save me and be with me always.

From now on bring me to shut my eyes, my heart, and my thoughts completely to this lowly world. Don't let me so much as glance at the vanities of this world, its temptations and distractions. This whole world is not worth the blink of an eye, "For all is vanity and torment of the spirit..." "...and what does man get out of all his labor?" (Ecclesiastes 1:14 and 1:3) — what does he get from all his desires and vanities?

O God: You are good and beneficent to everyone all the time. You are good and beneficent to the wicked as well as the good. Your goodness is true goodness. Show kindness to someone as far away as I am from Your true good, someone who has rebelled against Your goodness with my own hands, sometimes wilfully, sometimes unknowingly, sometimes deliberately and sometimes under compulsion, thousands and thousands of times. How many times You started giving me something good — true and eternal goodness — and I pushed it away with my very own hands. I've done this so many times I can't even count them any more.

Yet Your goodness never ceases. Please, God, from now on let me be a worthy recipient of Your true goodness. Satisfy me with Your eternal goodness and help me surrender myself to You until I become totally and absolutely merged in Your Unity — "running and returning" in the way we have been taught — until I come to know that everything is only for good, that there is no evil in the world at all, and that all the troubles and sufferings which come into the world are really all great benefits.

Grant insight!

Give us the ability to transcend all troubles and suffering this way, and receive any suffering that has to come to us with love and joy, transcending the pain through surrender to the ultimate goal, which is wholly good. Let us receive and draw forth the waters of Torah through the joy which comes from the trace that remains after this experience of surrender.

With our new Torah insights we will then be able to cool ourselves and ease our suffering, quenching the thirst of the soul even after we return from the state of surrender to our normal consciousness. Let the trace of the higher state which remains with us radiate to our conscious mind so as to bring us a vision of the secrets of the Torah. Then we will fulfill the teaching of the Psalms: "Happy is the man whom God disciplines and whom You teach from Your Torah" (Psalms 94:12).

Teach me to pray!

Loving God, help us to come to perfect prayer, and to make the whole prayer into one, so that all our prayers, our requests and entreaties will all be merged together in Your ultimate unity, and every day we will be able to sing and praise You and pray to You properly at length and ask You for everything we need.

Good and beneficent One: You desire the prayers of Your People, Israel. You know the great preciousness, the beauty, the splendor and the holiness of the words of the prayers we offer You. You know the glory, the radiance and the precious holiness of every single letter of the words of the prayers. For who is there who can do justice to the beauty and splendor of the precious garlands and treasured bouquets of flowers and blossoms that we gather from the supernal, holy fields, with every single sound and letter of our prayers, and every single utterance, not to speak of entire blessings and prayers?

If we were able to concentrate and listen to the precious pearls and jewels coming forth from our lips, if we were able to grasp the exalted glory and splendor of the awesomely holy words of the prayer and the preciousness of every single word, we would never be able to finish even a single blessing, or even a single word. We would be so tightly attached to the very first letter of the first word — because how can you possibly leave this letter behind when you see such beauty, such radiance and splendor? With such a powerful bond between the word and the soul, the word would never let the soul go any further!

Master of the World, in Your abundant loving kindness You have taught us that even when someone reaches such a level that they can actually hear the great beauty of each word, so that the word refuses to let them go further, this is also not good. This is still not perfect prayer — because a person has to say *all* the different blessings and prayers in order to complete the entire service. And even after the service is complete there are many additional requests, Psalms, and other prayers to be said.

I pray with my mouth, but my heart is far away

Perfect prayer is when we make the entire prayer into one unity, until it becomes merged in the ultimate goal, which is all goodness and unity. But God, You know what a low level we are on. You know how totally remote we are from these high spiritual goals. Our heads are so full of distractions, our hearts are so closed, that when we pray we hardly pay any attention at all to what our own mouths are saying.

I pray with my mouth and my lips, but my heart is far from the holy words, and I make virtually no effort to make my ears hear and attend to the words my mouth is saying. And even when You sometimes help me and I start hearing a faint echo of the message of one or other of the holy words of the prayer, I am still so totally removed from the goal of unity that I usually stay very attached to the one word I begin hearing, and I find it impossible to separate myself from it and continue with the prayer. I know that this is also not perfection, because I still have a lot more to say in order to complete the entire service, and to ask You for all the many things I need.

A fugitive and a wanderer

Because of all this I have come before You, Creator of everything, Master of all souls, to ask You to manifest Your love for the souls of Israel, and especially for my poor soul. I have sinned and rebelled against You again and again in all kinds of ways. For years and years my soul has been wandering in exile, far far away from the holy field where all the holy souls grow. My soul is a fugitive and a wanderer, a stranger, with no friends. No one knows her, no one recognizes her. She is just getting wilder and wilder, she is desperate. She finds no rest for the soles of her feet, "and all those who chase after her have caught up with her between the boundaries" (Lamentations 1:3).

My sins have caused all this, I know. But what should I do now? Were it not for Your loving kindness and tenderness I would be completely lost. I have let myself become enslaved by the evil impulse: how can the servant of one master speak with another Master? I am so far from my true soul: how can someone as wild and confused as I am speak the words of the living God? My only hope of coming back, my only hope of pleading for help, is through the true Master of the Field. This is what I come to plead with You for, my God and God of my fathers.

Send us the Master of the Field

I throw my entreaty before You, God of compassion, with a torn and broken heart, with anguish and trembling, mumbling and stuttering, hoping and longing for Your love and Your kindness, waiting in silence for Your help, which I know can come as quickly as the blink of an eye. I have no mouth to speak, I am too ashamed to lift up my head before You after all the wilful damage I have done through deliberately ignoring all the advice and guidance You have constantly showered upon me, and spurning all the good You have done for me. What justification do I still have to cry out to the King?

Even so, kind and loving God, show love to my soul and my spirit — my *nefesh*, my *ruach* and my *neshama* — for You alone know how pitiful they are after so many long days and years. Arouse Your love and compassion for my battered soul, and for all the naked souls who have sinned so much. What can I possibly say? How will I ever be able to repair all the damage I have done in such high places?

Have pity on our souls and the souls of all Your people the House of Israel, and on all the *neshamot, ruchot* and *nefashot* of the living and the dead. Send us the true Master of the Field who will work to restore our *nefashot, ruchot* and *neshamot* and all the souls of the living and the dead, and bring in all the souls from the outside back into the holy field, and attend to everything they need, sowing and planting, watering, tending and cultivating them so that their fruits will multiply, placing all the trees and plants at the correct distance so that none should overshadow and weaken any of the others.

"He turns the wilderness into a pool of water, and the parched land into a land of springs, and He settles the hungry there and they found a city of habitation. They sow fields and plant vineyards yielding abundant fruits. He blesses them and they multiply greatly and He does not let their cattle decrease" (Psalms 107:35-38).

Loving God, show love to all the true Tzaddikim — the Masters of the Field — who are working to repair the holy field: have pity on them and on all their descendents, on their followers and all who depend on them. Guard them and protect them from their enemies and all who hate and persecute them. You know the tremendous opposition they face, the terrible hatred and jealousy they encounter, the suffering and persecution they endure because of what they are trying to do. Call a halt to their troubles. Save and protect them. Give them life, strength and blessing, so that they will be able to do everything necessary to restore the Field and all our souls.

The naked souls

Show love to all those oppressed souls who are so many hundreds of years away from their tikkun. They have endured so many incarnations. They have gone through so much suffering in each one. Have pity on these tired, persecuted souls, and especially all the naked souls which cannot even be clothed in a body. You know how pitiful they are. Hear their cries, their weeping, their sighs and groans. See their bitter sorrow and distress — because their burdens are unbearable.

Have pity on them for Your Name's sake, and for the sake of Your abundant mercy. For we do not have the strength to pray for them and for us: we do not know how. Do it for Your sake and not for ours. Do not hold their sins against them, nor ours against us. "Hurry! Send Your love and kindness first, because we have fallen very low." Help us, because we are depending on You.

Bring us to complete repentance until the eyes of the Master of the Field radiate, and the Field will be the "Field of the Visionaries" and not the "Field of Weepers", God forbid. Give the Master of the Field the strength to see every single Jew who is still far from the goal and bring him to the truth, so that they will all be able to close their eyes and their minds to the mundane world completely and become completely merged in the true goal — "running and returning" — and every Jew will be able to make his prayer into a unity.

Beneficent God, help us to free ourselves of materialism completely until we are able to nullify ourselves totally and become wholly absorbed in Your unity at all times, so that our prayer will be merged in the ultimate unity from start to finish and we will never forget a single letter or word of our prayers. Even when we are standing at the end of the prayer, let us still remember the first letter and first word of the prayer, and never be separated from them even when we get to the end of the prayer. Never let the words of our prayers be separated and divided: let the entire prayer be entirely merged and bound up from beginning to end in the ultimate unity, the ultimate perfection.

And in this way let us be able to sing many songs of praise and offer many prayers day by day. Let us ask everything we need of You, confess all our sins, and speak words of reconciliation and endearment before You. Let us speak out the words clearly, and offer all our prayers sincerely and with concentration so that they will all be merged in complete unity with Your Holy Name. Hear our cry! Listen to our prayers and our entreaties! Fulfil all our requests for good, and help us to return to You quickly and completely. Let our place be with the Tzaddikim who sit before You in the Garden of Eden. Take delight in our souls for ever and ever, and give us the merit to live, and to see and inherit goodness and blessing in the time of Mashiach and in the life of the World to Come.

The Holy Dance

Help us to be happy at all times and give us the privilege of rising to see the dance of the Tzaddikim which is destined to take place in the future, when each one will point with his finger and say, "This is our God, we waited for Him!" — as it is written: "On that day it will be said, This is our God — we waited for Him and He saved us; this is HaShem — we waited for Him. We will be happy and rejoice over His salvation" (Isaiah 25:9). Whoever waits for this will be fortunate. Happy are those You choose and draw near, who will have the privilege of peeping out from the lattices to witness the joy of this dance.

God of love, Whose desire is to do good to all your creatures: show us love as long as our souls are in us. Give us life! Cleanse us, help us and save us. You know exactly what help we need to achieve speedily all the things we have asked of You, so that we will not come before You in shame.

"Let the words of my mouth and the meditation of my heart be acceptable before You, God, my Rock and my Redeemer. Rejoice in God and exult, Tzaddikim. Be happy, all who are upright in their heart. Let the Heavens rejoice and the Earth exult and let them say among the nations, HaShem rules." The day will come when "God will be King over all the earth. On that day God will be one and His Name One." And in Your Torah it is written: "Hear O Israel, HaShem our God, HaShem is One."

*

Accepting the Bad Things
Likutey Tefilot I:121

> "Happy is the person that God disciplines and whom You teach from Your Torah, to give him respite from the days of evil, until a pit is dug for the wicked. God will not cast off His people or forsake His heritage."
>
> Psalms 94:12-14

Master of the World. God of love and goodness. Help me to be able to bear everything with love — even when Your love for me necessitates Your sending me suffering that to my eyes seems evil, God forbid. Let me bear everything with genuine love. Open my heart and help me grow in holiness until I really come to know and understand that, considering the person I am and all I have done against You, everything You do to me is done with infinite kindness and mercy. It would be quite impossible to ever describe or explain the overwhelming love and goodness You have shown me in the past and the present, and that I know You are going to show me in the future. "What can I give God in return after all the kindness He has shown me?" (Psalms 116:12)

But what can I do? My sins have closed up my heart, and my understanding is distorted. I do not *feel* Your love in my heart. On the contrary, I find myself constantly questioning Your good and righteous ways. This is why I have come before

You now — to pour out my heart and beg You to keep me from all such twisted ideas, and strengthen my faith and awareness of You. Let me always know and believe that You are just and Your judgements are fair. Let me recognize that, considering all the wrong I have done, You always treat me with infinite mercy and tenderness.

And I ask You to take pity on me and guard and protect me from all evil, pain and suffering. Because You are gracious and abundant to forgive. I have sinned so much that all the suffering in the world would be insufficient to make amends for even one of my sins. Yet You have the power to forgive and grant pardon with no suffering whatsover, "For forgiveness is with You, in order that You may be feared... for with God is kindness, and with Him is abundant redemption. And He will redeem Israel from all their sins." (Psalms 130:4, 7-8).

And so I stretch out my hand to You, Master of love: show me Your love, guard my soul, and save me from every kind of evil, pain and suffering in the world. Don't treat us according to our sins and transgressions. Whatever Your love and mercy may require us to bear, please, good and beneficent God, work wonders with us for the sake of life, and help us to bear it with perfect, genuine love. Don't ever send me suffering except if You help me to bear it with perfect love. Don't let me ever even start to question Your ways — let me always know that I myself must take responsibility for the wrong I have done.

For Your sake have mercy on me and let me not rebel and kick when I have to suffer. Give me the strength and understanding to accept my suffering with love if ever You wish to discipline me lovingly, like a father disciplines his child. Take pity on me and lighten the burden of my suffering in every way possible. Because I am weak, my understanding is limited, and I do not have the strength or understanding to bear suffering at all. "Be gracious to me, O God: in Your mercy and loving kindness, blot out my sins." "In Your kindness, give me life, and I will guard the testimony of Your mouth." "O God, do not chastise me with anger or discipline me in Your wrath."

Loving God, let my will be Your will — let me surrender my will completely to Yours and have no will other than Yours. Let my will be only that everything should be according to Your will from now and for ever. Amen.

*

The Problem Contains Its Own Solution
Likutey Tefilot I:133

"Answer me when I call, God of my righteousness. In my distress You relieved me. Be gracious to me and hear my prayer."

Psalms 4:2

God of love and goodness:

Help me, purify me, open my heart and deepen my understanding so that I will always be able to see the goodness and help You send, even in times of great difficulty and trouble. Your help is the only thing that keeps me alive and enables me to stand up under the pressure of all my troubles. I have pressures on all sides, materially and spiritually. Wherever I try to move I find obstacles. Worst of all, I don't even know where to go to escape from my own self. Because I know that I myself am the main cause of everything I'm going through, because of my sins and bad behavior, my bad thoughts and attitudes.

Yet even so You have still not held back Your kindness from me. "God's kindnesses are never finished, and His love is never exhausted" (Lamentations 3:22). "For Your love for me has been very great, and You have saved my soul from the lowest hell" (Psalms 86:13). Every day and every moment Your kindness to me has been so very great — it is awesome and amazing. If not for Your kindness at all times I would long ago have been finished.

And just because Your love and mercy are so very great, help me to see, to recognize and *feel* Your constant goodness and kindness at all times. Help me to find and recognize the many different ways You have of helping me even in and through my very troubles and problems. Then I'll be able to be happy at all times, because I'll know You are helping me. I'll be spiritually strong and able to pray to You constantly no matter what happens. I'll be able to thank You at all times for all that You have done for me in the past, and cry out to You for help in whatever is to come. And I will never have the slightest doubts about the justice and fairness of Your ways. No matter what happens to me and the whole Jewish People, I will be able to believe with perfect faith that You are just and fair, because You run the world with kindness and deal with Your creatures with love: "God is good to all and his love is over all His works" (Psalms 145:9).

Kind and loving God, take pity on us and drive away all the crooked thoughts in our hearts. Let us never entertain even the slightest doubts about the way You treat us. Let me only see Your help and salvation and the wonderful kindness and goodness You send at all times. Even in the middle of troubles and difficulties, God forbid, You have the most amazing ways of sending help and relief of all kinds — besides the fact that we are constantly hoping and expecting that You will quickly release us from all our troubles and sorrows and send complete salvation.

Loving Father. You show mercy to the poor and save in times of trouble. In this present time of trouble and crisis, let Your love for us be aroused. Answer us, God, answer us, because we are in great trouble. Rock of Israel, rise up to help Your people, Israel. Don't let our faith waver in the midst of everything we are going through during these hard times. You know how bitter are the troubles afflicting the Jewish People. Our difficulties are getting worse and worse, and the problems are spreading further and further afield. We have been driven to the point where many are wavering in their faith and have doubts and questions about Your ways. We have no one to stand up for us.

Have pity on us for the sake of Your Name. Look upon us in our suffering. The pain of our heart is so great. Guardian of Israel, protect the remnant of Israel, and show love and pity for every single Jewish soul, so that not a single one should fall away from holy faith because of what is happening now to the Jewish People. On the contrary, let the present situation make us stronger and stir us to return to You sincerely with all our hearts. We will pray and entreat and cry out to You until You answer us, and we will know and believe in the truth — that You will never ever abandon us. "For God will not cast off His people, and He will not abandon His inheritance" (Psalms 94:14). "For God will not cast off His people, for the sake of His great Name, for God wished to make you His people" (I Samuel 12:22).

Help us, God of our salvation, for the sake of the glory of Your name. Save us and atone for our sins for the sake of Your name. May the words of my mouth and the meditation of my heart be acceptable before You O God my Rock and my Redeemer.

*